D1253815

SACRED WISDOM

CHINESE
WISDOM

The Way of Perfect Harmony

Edited by
Gerald Benedict

Introduction by
Stephan Schuhmacher

WATKINS PUBLISHING
LONDON

This anthology of *Chinese Wisdom* has been
selected by Gerald Benedict

This edition produced in 2010 for Sacred Wisdom,
an imprint of Watkins Publishing
Sixth Floor, Castle House, 75–76 Wells Street, London W1T 3QH
Distributed in the United States and Canada by
Sterling Publishing Co., Inc.
387 Park Avenue South, New York, NY 10016-8810

First published in the UK in 2009

Copyright © Watkins Publishing,
a division of Duncan Baird Publishers 2009

Sacred Wisdom design copyright © Duncan Baird Publishers
Introduction copyright © Stephan Schuhmacher

All rights reserved in this edition. This publication may not
be reproduced, stored in a retrieval system or transmitted in
any form or by any means, electronic, mechanical,
photocopying, recording or otherwise, without prior
permission in writing from the publishers

1 3 5 7 9 10 8 6 4 2

Designed in Great Britain by Jerry Goldie
Printed and bound in India by Imago

Library of Congress Cataloging-in-Publication data available

ISBN: 978-1-906787-44-8

www.watkinspublishing.co.uk

CONTENTS

AUTHOR'S NOTE

The separator used between the entries of the text is the Chinese character for Tao:

道

The number in brackets following each source refers to the number in References at the back.

The author has made every effort to secure permission to reproduce material protected by copyright, and will be pleased to make good any omissions brought to his attention in future printings of this book.

INTRODUCTION

All wisdom teachings aspire to remind us that a state of perfect harmony is attainable for human beings despite, and from within, their human predicament, and directions are given as to how this harmony can be actualized. The wisdom teachings that are rooted in the dualistic consciousness of the Mediterranean cultures and their religions (Judaism, Christianity and Islam) place the attainability of this paradisiacal state in some kind of otherworldly 'hereafter' or 'beyond', and therefore tend towards metaphysical speculation. Eastern wisdom, on the other hand, affirms that this harmony of the heart-mind can be attained and is inherent in our present secular existence.

The Chinese are said to be a very pragmatic people (about which there's no doubt if one looks at their proficiency in business), and thus their approach to wisdom and perfect harmony also has been very practical and down-to-earth. Leaving metaphysical speculation aside, this approach is, in Western terms, more of a 'science', since it is based on the observation of nature and its laws. From millennia of observation of the processes in nature the Chinese sages have deduced that there is but one constant in our world – and that is *change*. The path to the realization of harmony – within oneself, with other people, and with the whole universe – is the understanding of the patterns of change, and the acceptance of and adaptation to the inevitable constant change in life.

The 'laws' of change have been distilled into one of the oldest wisdom books of mankind, the Chinese classic *I Ching*, whose roots are said to go back 8,000 years into Chinese prehistory. The 64 hexagrams of the *I Ching* represent the basic patterns and qualities of change, the change that comes about as a result of the interaction of the two fundamental polar qualities in the universe: Yin (dark, female, receptive, negative) and Yang (light, male, active, positive). For the Chinese, the human being as the microcosm, and the universe as the macrocosm, are governed by the same laws of change ('As above, so below' is no invention of hermetic philosophy), and so the *I Ching* is claimed by the two great indigenous schools of Chinese thought, Taoism and Confucianism, as a 'classic' of their own tradition.

What is called 'Chinese Wisdom' today is basically
the teachings of these two indigenous Chinese
traditions, and of a third tradition, the teachings of
Buddhism, imported into China via the silk road.
Buddhism, which in India was slowly superseded by
Hinduism from the 10th century onward and later
practically eradicated by Islam, came to a new heyday
in China. Chinese Buddhism reflected the whole range
of Buddhist thought in the metaphysical teachings of
the Hua-yen school, the syncretistic T'ien-t'ai school,
the earthy wisdom of the Ch'an school, the popular
eschatological teachings of the Pure Land school and
the Chinese adaptation of the Tibetan Vajrayâna in the
Mi-tsung school.

Ch'an, which later was called Zen in Japan, proved
to be the most vital and culturally the most influen-
tial school of Chinese Buddhism. Many people in the
West think that Zen Buddhism originated in Japan and
are not aware that Zen is an offspring and the Japanese
denomination of Chinese Ch'an. Also few people in the
West are aware that Ch'an/Zen is not purely of
Buddhist origin, but would not have been possible in
its typical form without the indigenous Chinese
Taoism. The basics of Indian Meditation Buddhism
(one of the parents of Ch'an) were so kindred to the
basic philosophy of Taoism, that early Chinese Ch'an

Buddhists. They assert that harmony cannot be enforced on people from the outside; for harmony to radiate outwards, it has to be inwardly actualized. For Ch'an, the most radical of mystical schools in China, the holy scriptures and religious and philosophical systems are at best a finger that points at the moon of wisdom; they are never wisdom itself, never an end in itself. The only reliable authority for the mystics is the evidence of their own direct experience of ultimate reality. They avoid calling this ultimate reality 'holy', as a way of correcting the tendency of dualistic thinking, which maintains a distinction between sacred and profane. And since they do not rely on holy scripture, and do not need the intervention of priests and political or religious institutions to find perfect harmony, they are often ... well, to say the least ... *challenged* by the priests and institutions that are 'in power'.

The esoteric schools tend to regard the human being as basically good. This basic goodness cannot be brought about by rules and methods; it cannot be *made*, since it is always already at hand. Thus Buddhist schools affirm that human beings are inherently perfect, that they possess (or as Ch'an would rather say, they *are*) Buddha Nature, and all that is needed to manifest their inherent perfect harmony is to realize is, in many cases, a restatement of Meditation Buddhism in Taoist terms. Ch'an-Buddhism never lost its Taoist flavour.

Beyond the distinction of all these different schools of thought, the texts collected in this volume mirror the basic distinction between exoteric and esoteric schools of thought, which we find in all ages and all cultures. The exoteric schools are usually based on the authority of 'holy' scriptures, or the doctrines of venerated teachers, which must be adhered to 'to the letter'. The exoteric schools in China (Confucianism with all its offspring) tend to believe in the education-al power of the human intellect and try to 'fix' human beings and society from the outside in. Their means for 'bettering' the world are rules and regulations, and religious and political dogmas. Compliance to these rules is often assured by the sanctions of government or religious institutions. The exoteric schools tend to see mankind, or at least their contemporaries, as basically evil, 'fallen' from the state of perfect harmony that existed 'in the beginning', or in prehistoric times. They are convinced that this harmony can only be regained by strict adherence to their own rules and institutions.

The philosophical antipodes to the 'exoterics' are the 'esoterics' or mystics, in China the Taoists and this perfection beyond the point of distinguishing between perfection and imperfection. For the Taoists, it is exactly the belief in the necessity of *doing*, of employing means, methods, rules, systems, which inhibits the realization and actualization of basic goodness. The attempts of the Confucians to educate and improve people are, for Taoists such as Lao Tzu or Chuang Tzu, activities that distort basic and natural goodness, turning it into some kind of socially accepted, but *artificial* decorum which runs against nature. And since man, the microcosm, cannot realize perfect harmony by contradicting nature, the macrocosm, the Taoists advocate the path of not-doing (*wu wei*) as the Way to the perfect harmony. This harmony lies in being spontaneously (*tzu-jan*) in accord with the ultimate nature of the Tao, the unchanging, as well as with the constant changes manifested as the phenomenal world out of the vast emptiness of the Tao.

Stephan Schuhmacher
the 'Abode of the White Clouds'
France, 2009

CHINESE WISDOM

The Way of Perfect Harmony

Books are what the world values as representing Tao. But books are only words, and the valuable part of words is the thought therein contained. That thought has a certain bias which cannot be conveyed in words, yet the world values words as being the essence of books. But though the world values them, they are not of value; as that sense in which the world values them is not the sense in which they are valuable.

Chuang Tzu, 4th century BCE (1)

ON ORIGINS AND BEGINNINGS

The World Has a Beginning

The world has a beginning

that is the mother of the world.

Once you've found the mother,

thereby you know the child.

Once you know the child,

you return to keep the mother,

not perishing though the body die.

Close your eyes, shut your doors,

and you do not toil all your life.

Open your eyes, carry out your affairs,

and you are not saved all your life.

Seeing the small is called clarity,

keeping flexible is called strength.

Using the shining radiance,

you return again to the light,

not leaving anything to harm yourself.

This is called entering the eternal.

Lao Tzu, 6th century BCE (2)

The Beginnings of Reality

There was a beginning. There was a time before that beginning. There was a time before the time which was before the beginning. There was being. There was non-being. There was a time before that non-being. There was a time before the time which was before that non-being.

What is meant by 'There was a beginning' is that there was accumulation which has not sprung into activity. There were signs of sprouts and shoots but no physical form. Like insects moving, they are about to spring into life but their species have not yet been formed.

At the time before the beginning, the material force (*ch' i*) of Heaven began to descend and that of Earth began to ascend. Yin and Yang interacted and united, competing leisurely to expand in the universe.

The Huai-Nan Tzu, 2nd century BCE (3)

道

Existence is beyond the power
  of words to define.

Terms may be used

But none of them are absolute.

In the beginning of heaven and earth
  there were no words,

Words came out of the womb of matter;

And whether a man dispassionately

[10]

Sees to the core of life

Or passionately

Sees the surface

They are essentially the same,

Words making them seem different

Only to express appearance.

If name be needed, wonder names them both:

From wonder into wonder

Existence opens.

Lao Tzu, 6th century BCE (4)

The Energy of Tao

It is through Tao that the stars and the earth move, that processes of change go on without end, and that water flows without stopping; for Tao is the beginning and end of all creation. The rising of wind, the gathering of clouds, are as they should be; so too the rolling of thunder, the fall of rain, and so on, without end.

The operations of Tao are mysterious. They resemble the actions of the potter, whose wheel forever goes round and round. In the natural succession of change, creations are finished and polished, and afterwards dissolve again into their pristine elements.

Those who do not interfere and leave nothing undone are in harmony with Tao; those who speak with care understand power; those who know tranquillity and are content, devoid of conceit, are in possession of harmony, even though they live in the midst of a myriad diversities. All things are in accordance with their various natures.

The energy of Tao operates in the smallest thing and yet compels the mighty universe. Its power moulds the universe and harmonizes the masculine and feminine, the light and the dark; it forms the four seasons and brings the elements of nature into accord.

The Huai-Nan Tzu, 2nd century BCE (5)

There was something formlessly fashioned,

That existed before heaven and earth,

Without sound, without substance,

Dependent on nothing, unchanging,

All pervading, unfailing.

One may think of it as the mother of all things
under heaven.

Its true name we do not know;

'Way' is the by-name we give it.

Lao Tzu, 6th century BCE (4)

Cause and Effect in Action

If you plant wheat, you get wheat; if you plant
flax, you get flax. Flax does not produce wheat,
wheat does not produce flax – the seeds are
different.

What I realise as I observe this is the Tao of
cause and effect in action. If people's thought is
good, their actions and deeds are good, so they

will surely receive a blessing. If people's thought is bad, their actions and deeds are also bad, so they will surely bring on misfortune. ...

◊ Where there is a cause, it will surely have an effect.

Liu I-Ming, 18th century CE (6)

道

The Tao that can be trodden is not the
    enduring and unchanging Tao.

The name that can be named is not the
    enduring and unchanging name.

(Conceived of as) having no name, it is the
    Originator of heaven and earth;

(conceived of as) having a name, it is the
    Mother of all things.

Lao Tzu, 6th century BCE (7)

It is only the Sage who can relate the myriad things to the One and tie it to the origin. If the source is not traced and the development from it not followed, nothing can be accomplished. ... The origin is the same as the source. It means that if man in his life has a beginning and end like this, he does not have to respond to the changes of the four seasons. Therefore the origin is the source of all things, and the origin of man is found in it.

Tung Chung-Shu, 179–104 BCE (8)

道

Existence by nothing bred,

Breeds everything.

Parent of the universe,

It smoothes rough edges,

Unties hard knots,

Tempers the sharp sun,

Lays blowing dust,

Its image in the wellspring never fails.

But how was it conceived? – this image

Of no other sire.

Lao Tzu, 6th century BCE (4)

Mind is the Origin of All Things

The mind is the root from which all things grow. If you can understand the mind, everything else is included. It's like the root of a tree. All a tree's fruit and flowers, branches and leaves depend on its root. If you nourish its root, a tree multiplies. If you cut its roots, it dies. Those who understand the mind reach enlightenment with minimal effort. Those who don't understand the mind practice in vain. Everything good and bad comes from your own mind. To find something beyond the mind is impossible.

Bodhidharma, 5th century BCE (9)

What preceded life?

The earth.

What preceded the earth?

The universe.

What preceded the universe?

The soundless and shapeless

origin of origins,

ever transforming

and having no beginning nor end.

This Mother of the universe

is boundless and nameless.

But if we want to share with you

anything about this remarkable

non-existing executor,

we must invent a name for it.

We will call it the *Tao*

because Tao means *great*.

Incredibly great

because it occupies infinite space,

being fully present in the whole
  universe,

and in every infinitesimal particle.

Because the Tao

created the universe,

and the universe created the earth

and the earth created us,

we are all incredibly great.

Lao Tzu, 6th century BCE (10)

道

Hexagram 1:
Ch'ien (Heaven) –
The Creative Principle

THE TRIGRAMS

above: Ch'ien – Heaven, the Creative
below: Ch'ien – Heaven, the Creative

Ch'ien represents what is great, penetrating, advantageous, correct and firm. It is the originator, the creative. The hexagram consists entirely of yang lines, with the qualities of creativity, virility, activity and strength.

The Judgement: Ch'ien works sublime success. Perseverance brings favourable results to he who is firm and unyielding.

Commentary: Vast is the great originator. All things owe their being to it, and it contains all the meanings embodied in its name: the clouds move and the rain falls everywhere; all things appear in their developed form. Ch'ien transforms everything, developing its true nature as heaven determines, preserving great harmony in union.

The Image: The movement of the heavens reveals transcendent power. The superior man, therefore, nerves himself to untiring activity.

I Ching, written during the Zhou dynasty, 1122–256 BCE (11)

– 2 –

ON LIFE AND BEING
HUMAN

◈ A man who knows that he is a fool
is not a great fool.

Chuang Tzu, 4th century BCE (1)

道

A sage said, 'If for one day you can master yourself and return to considerate behaviour, the
whole world will return to humanity.' Do you
think humanity depends on yourself or on others?

Liu I-Ming, 18th century CE (12)

Men knowing the way of life

Do without acting,

Effect without enforcing,

Taste without consuming;

Through the many they find the few,

Through the humble the great.

They respect their foes,

They face the simple fact before it becomes
   involved.

Solve the small problem before it becomes big.

The most involved fact in the world

Could have been faced when it was simple,

The biggest problem in the world

Could have been solved when it was small.

The simple fact that he finds no problem big

Is a sane man's prime achievement.

If you say yes too quickly

You may have to say no,

If you think things are done easily

You may find them hard to do:

If you face trouble sanely

It cannot trouble you.

Lao Tzu, 6th century BCE (4)

道

It is not truth that makes man great, but man that makes truth great.

Confucius, 551–479 BCE (13)

道

The philosopher Tsang said, 'I daily examine myself on three points: whether, in transacting business for others, I may have been not faithful; whether, in intercourse with friends, I may have been not sincere; whether I may have not mastered and practiced the instructions of my teacher.'

Confucius, 551–479 BCE (14)

Sincere Thoughts

What is meant by 'making the thoughts sincere', is allowing no self-deception, as when we hate a bad smell, and as when we love what is beautiful. This is called self-enjoyment. Therefore, the superior man must be watchful over himself when he is alone. There is no evil to which the mean man … will not proceed, but when he sees a superior man, he instantly tries to disguise himself, concealing his evil, and displaying what is good.

The other beholds him, as if he saw his heart and veins – of what use is his disguise? This is an instance of the saying 'What truly is within will be manifested without'. Therefore, the superior man must be watchful over himself when he is alone.

Confucius, 551–479 BCE (15)

Cultivation of the Person

What is meant by 'The cultivation of the person depends on rectifying the mind' may be thus illustrated: If a man be under the influence of passion he will be incorrect in his conduct. He will be the same, if he is under the influence of terror, or under the influence of fond regard, or under that of sorrow and distress. When the mind is not present, we look and do not see; we hear and do not understand; we eat and do not know the taste of what we eat. This is what is meant by saying that the cultivation of the person depends on the rectifying of the mind.

Confucius, 551–479 BCE (15)

Returning to Live in the Country 2

I always loved to walk the woods and
   mountains,

Pleased myself, lost in fields and marshes.

Now I go out with nephews, nieces,

In the wilds, parting hazel branches,

Back and forth through the mounds and
  hollows,

All around us signs of ancient peoples,

Remnants of their broken hearths and well-
  heads,

Mulberry and bamboo groves neglected.

Stop and ask the simple woodsman,

'Where have all these people gone now?'

Turning he looks quietly and tells me,

'Nothing's left of them, they're finished.'

One world. Though the lives we lead are
  different,

In courts of power or labouring in the market,

These I know are more than empty words:

Our life's a play of light and shade,

Returning at last to the Void.

T'ao Chi'en, 365–427 (16)

Because of desire and craving, stress and anxiety arise. Because there is anxiety and stress, body and mind are afflicted by tensions.

Lao Tzu, 6th century BCE (4)

Vitality and Consciousness

Carrying vitality and consciousness,

embracing them as one,

can you keep them from parting?

Concentrating energy,

making it supple,

can you be like an infant?

Purifying hidden perception,

can you make it flawless?

Loving the people, governing the nation,

can you be uncontrived?

As the gate of heaven opens and closes,

can you be impassive?

Producing and developing,

producing without possessing,

doing without presuming,

growing without domineering:

this is called mysterious power.

Lao Tzu, 6th century BCE (2)

The Pupil of the Eye

Of all the parts of a man, there is none more excellent than the pupil of the eye. It cannot conceal wickedness. If within the breast all is correct, the pupil is bright; if not, it is dull. Listen to a man's words and look at the pupil of his eye; how can a man hide his character?

Mencius, 371–289 BCE (17)

道

Don't be surprised, don't be startled; all things will arrange themselves. Don't cause a disturbance, don't exert pressure; all things will clarify themselves.

The Huai-Nan Tzu, 2nd century BCE (3)

On Living in General

Passion holds up the bottom of the universe and genius paints up its roof.

Better be insulated by common people than be despised by gentlemen; better be flunked by an official examination than be unknown to a famous scholar.

A man should so live as to be like a poem, and a thing should so look as to be like a picture.

To be born in times of peace in a district with hills and lakes when the magistrate is just and upright, and to live in a family of comfortable means, marry an understanding wife and have intelligent sons – this is what I call perfect life.

To sit alone on a quiet night – to invite the moon and tell her one's sorrows; to keep alone on a good night – and to call the insects and tell them one's regrets.

Wine can take the place of tea, but tea cannot take the place of wine; poems can take the place of prose, but prose cannot take the place of poems; ... the moon can take the place of lamps, but lamps cannot take the place of the moon; the pen can take the place of the mouth, but the mouth cannot take the place of the pen.

It is easy to stand a pain, but difficult to stand an itch; it is easy to bear the bitter taste, but difficult to bear the sour taste. ...

The stork gives a man the romantic manner, the horse gives a man the heroic manner, the orchid gives a man the recluse's manner, and the pine gives a man the grand manner of the ancients.

It is against the will of God to eat delicate food hastily, to pass gorgeous views hurriedly, to express deep sentiments superficially, to pass a beautiful day steeped in food and drinks, and to enjoy your wealth steeped in luxuries.

Ch'ang Ch'ao, 17th century CE (18)

Real words are not vain,

Vain words not real;

And since those who argue prove nothing

A sensible man is wiser than he knows,

While a fool knows more than is wise.

Therefore a sensible man does not devise
  resources:

The greater his use to others

The greater their use to him,

The more he yields to others

The more they yield to him.

The way of life cleaves without cutting:

Which, without need to say,

Should be man's way.

Lao Tzu, 6th century BCE (4)

If you adopt, as absolute, a standard of evenness which is so only relatively, your results will not be absolutely even. If you adopt, as absolute, a criterion of right which is so only relatively, your results will not be absolutely right. Those who trust to their senses become slaves to objective existences. Those alone who are guided by their intuitions find the true standard. So far are the senses less reliable than the intuitions. Yet fools trust to their senses to know what is good for mankind, with, alas, but external results.

Chuang Tzu, 4th century BCE (1)

道

When mortals are alive, they worry about death. When they're full, they worry about hunger. Theirs is the Great Uncertainty.

But sages don't consider the past. ?And they don't worry about the future. Nor do they cling to the present. And from moment to moment they follow the Way.

Bodhidharma, 5th century CE (19)

Whatever has a body assumes form and so must disintegrate. Whatever has energy is born and so must die. This body and energy are the basis of becoming and disintegration, birth and death.

What I realise as I observe this is the Tao of shedding birth and death.

⌈Perfected human beings transform the temporal and restore the primal. They rest their bodies in open space, store their spirits in silent tranquillity. Uninvolved with the energy of the five forces, they are unmoved by myriad things. ... Heaven and earth cannot constrain them, Creation cannot rule them.⌉

Liu I-Ming, 18th century CE (6)

道

⌈If you live in disappointment and anxiety you *yes!* will sink into the ocean of suffering and forever stray from the True Way.⌉

Lao Tzu, 6th century BCE (20)

To be angry is to let others' mistakes
punish yourself.

Amen!

To forgive others is to be good to yourself.

Cheng Yen, b. 1937 (19)

道

The body is the house of life; energy is the basis
of life; spirit is the controller of life: if one loses
its position, all three are injured. Therefore when
the spirit is in the lead, the spirit follows
beneficial results; when the body is in the lead,
the spirit follows it with harmful results. Those
people whose lives are gluttony and lust are
tripped and blinded by power and profit, seduced
and charmed by fame and status, nearly beyond
human conception. *Indeed!*

Lao Tzu, 6th century BCE (20)

When the vitality, spirit, will and energy are calm, they fill you day by day and make you strong. When they are hyperactive, they are depleted day by day, making you old.

Therefore the sages keep nurturing their spirit, make their energy gentle, make their bodies normal, and bob with the Way. In this way they keep company with the evolution of all things and respond to the Ch'an sages in all events. ...

So the physical body may pass away, but the spirit does not change. Use the unchanging to respond to changing, and there is never any limit. What changes returns to formlessness, while what does not change lives together with the universe.

So what gives birth to life is not itself born; what it gives birth to is what is born. What produces change does not itself change; what it changes is what changes. This is where real people roam, the path of quintessence.

Lao Tzu, 6th century BCE (20)

Developing One's Human Nature

Human nature is developed by profound serenity and lightness, virtue is developed by harmonious joy and open selflessness. When externals do not confuse you inwardly, your nature finds the condition that suits it; when your nature does not disturb harmony, virtue rests in its place.

If you can get through life in the world by developing your nature and embrace virtue to the end of your years, it can be said that you are able to embody the Tao.

The Huai-Nan Tzu, 2nd century BCE (3)

Self-Confidence

'What I point out to you is only that you shouldn't allow yourselves to be confused by others. Act when you need to, without further hesitation or doubt. People today can't do this ... what is the affliction? Their affliction is their lack of self-confidence. If you do not spontaneously trust yourself sufficiently, you will be in a frantic state, pursuing all sorts of objects, unable to be independent.'

⌈We can only learn by admitting we don't know everything yet, we can only grow if we accept that we are not perfect, just like everyone else around us.

Be light, humorous, eager to learn, courageous to change and not afraid of making mistakes.

Amen! Emotionally beating yourself up is not helping yourself or the world; it does not change the past, nor does it change the future; it only makes the present miserable.⌋

Ch'an Master Linji, 9th century CE (19)

A Parting

The river rolls crystal as clear as the sky,

To blend far away with the blue waves of the
  ocean;

Man alone, when the hour of departure is nigh,

With a wine-cup can soothe his emotion.

The birds of the valley sing loud in the sun,

Where the gibbons their vigils will shortly be
 keeping:

I thought that with tears I had long ago done,

But now I shall never cease weeping.

Li Po, 705–62 (21)

道

To the mind that is still, the whole universe
 surrenders.

To know, yet to think that one does not know
 is best;

Not to know, yet to think that one knows will
 lead to difficulty.

Original nature can intuit all happenings.

In original nature is the essence of goodness.

Be natural in your actions and you will always
 be pure and still.

Lao Tzu, 6th century BCE (3)

[38]

Kindness in words creates confidence.

Kindness in thinking creates profoundness.

Kindness in giving creates love.

Knowing others is intelligence; knowing
    yourself is true wisdom.

Mastering others is strength, mastering
    yourself is true power.

Fill your bowl to the brim and it will spill.

Keep sharpening your knife and it
    will blunt.

Chase after money and security and your heart
    will never unclench.

Care about other people's approval and you will
    be their prisoner.

Do your work, then step back. The only path to
    serenity.

Lao Tzu, 6th century BCE (7)

Peaceful Old Age

Chuang Tzu said: 'Tao gives me this toil in
    manhood,

this repose in old age, this rest in death.'

Swiftly and soon the golden sun goes down,

The blue sky lingers far into the night.

Tao is the changeful world's environment;

Happy are they that in its laws delight.

Tao gives me toil, youth's passion to achieve,

And leisure in life's autumn and decay.

I follow Tao – the seasons are my friends;

Opposing it misfortunes come my way.

Within my breast no sorrows can abide;

I feel the great world's spirit through me thrill,

And as a cloud I drift before the wind,

Or with the random swallow take my will.

As underneath the mulberry-tree I dream,

The water-clock drips on, and dawn appears:

A new day shines on wrinkles and white hair,

The symbols of the fullness of my years.

If I depart, I cast no look behind:

Still wed to life, I still am free from care.

Since life and death in cycles come and go,

Of little moments are the days to spare.

Thus strong in faith I wait, and long to be

One with the pulsings of Eternity.

Po Chu-I, 772–846 (22)

道

The fish trap exists because of the fish; once you've caught the fish, you can forget the trap. The rabbit snare exists because of the rabbit; once you've caught the rabbit, you can forget the snare. Words exist because of their meaning; once you have grasped the meaning, you can forget the words. Where can I find a man who has forgotten words so I can have a word with him?

Chuang Tzu, 4th century BCE (1)

An Answer to Sub-Prefect Zhang

In these late years stillness is all my concern,

The world's business does not bother my heart
any more.

Gaze turned inward, there are no major plans.

Empty of knowledge, return to my original
home.

Wind in the pine trees, my loosened sash
billows,

Moon over mountains enlightens my zither play.

You ask what's my view of failure and success —

The fisherman's song comes from the far
  riverbank.

Wang Wei, 698–759 (23)

Ninth Day, Ninth Month

Slowly autumn comes to an end.

Painfully cold a dawn wind licks the dew.

Grass round here will not be green again,

Trees and leaves are already suffering.

The clear air is drained and purified

And the high white sky's a mystery.

Nothing's left of the cicada's sound.

Flying geese break the heavens' silence.

The Myriad Creatures rise and return.

How can life and death not be hard?

From the beginning all things have to die.

Thinking of it can bruise the heart.

What can I do to lighten my thoughts?

Solace myself drinking the last of this wine.

Who understands the next thousand years?

Let's just make this morning last forever.

T'ao Ch'ien, 365–427 (16)

The Nature of Man

Yang Chu said, 'Men resemble heaven and earth in that they cherish five virtues. [Benevolence, uprightness, propriety, knowledge, and good faith.] Of all creatures, man is the most skilful. His nails and teeth do not suffice to procure him maintenance and shelter. His skin and sinews do not suffice to defend him; though running he cannot attain profit nor escape harm, and he has neither hair nor feathers to protect him from the cold and heat. He is thus compelled to use things to nourish his nature, to rely on his intelligence, and not to put his confidence in brute force; therefore intelligence is appreciated because it preserves us and brute force is despised because it encroaches upon things.

'But I am not the owner of my own body, for I, when I am born, must complete it; nor do I possess things, for having got them, I must part with them again. The body is essential for birth, but things are essential for its maintenance. If there were a body born complete I could not possess it, and I could not possess things not to be parted with. For possessing a body or things would be unlawfully appropriating a body belonging to the whole universe, and appropriating things belonging to the universe no sage would do.

'He who regards as common property a body appertaining to the universe and the things of the universe is a perfect man. And that is the highest degree of perfection.'

Yang Chu, c. 3rd century BCE (24)

道

Spiritual Rigor Mortis

The more people try to use willpower to obliterate a desire, the more they strengthen the desire. The additional force only serves to confuse them. They become obsessed with the problem. The more people talk about the Dharma without knowing what it is, the more they strengthen their ignorance. They grow in this ignorance and soon consider themselves towers of rectitude. They're like fish out of water who attempt to teach others to swim, or like caged birds who offer lessons in flying.

If you want to conquer a desire, take off its mask and see it for what it is. Instantly, it becomes insignificant and not worth a second thought. ... Familiarize yourself with human nature by recognizing your own errors and base desires. Instantly, you'll forgive others for their mistakes. Be humble and gentle in your love for humanity. That's the way to set an example for others to copy.

Proud rigidity isn't rectitude. It's spiritual rigor mortis.

Han Shan, 1546–1623 (25)

He who is open-eyed is open-minded,

He who is open-minded is open-hearted,

He who is open-hearted is kingly,

He who is kingly is godly,

He who is godly is useful,

He who is useful is infinite,

He who is infinite is immune,

He who is immune is immortal.

Lao Tzu, 6th century BCE (4)

道

Probably the Creator knew well that, when he created man upon the earth, he was producing a scamp, a brilliant scamp, it is true, but a scamp nonetheless The scamp-like qualities of man are, after all, his most hopeful qualities. This scamp that the creator has produced is undoubtedly a brilliant chap. He is still a very unruly and awkward adolescent, thinking himself greater and wiser than he really is, still full of mischief and naughtiness and love of a free-for-all. Nevertheless, there is so much good in him that the Creator might still be willing to pin on him his hopes, as a father sometimes pins his hopes on a brilliant but somewhat erratic son of twenty. Would he be willing some day to retire and turn over the management of this universe to this erratic son of his? I wonder …

Lin Yutang, 1895–1976 (26)

Any good practical philosophy must start out with the recognition of our having a body. It is high time that some among us made the straight admission that we are animals, an admission which is inevitable since the establishment of the basic truth of the Darwinian theory. … The men of the spirit were as proud of the spirit as the shoemaker is proud of the leather. Sometimes even the spirit was not sufficiently remote and abstract and they had to use words like 'essence' or 'soul' or 'idea'. … The human body was distilled in this scholastic machine into a spirit.

This over-emphasis on the spirit was fatal. It made us war with our natural instincts. Man is made of flesh and spirit both, and it should be philosophy's business to see the mind and body live harmoniously together, that there be reconciliation between the two.

Lin Yutang, 1895–1976 (26)

道

Those who pursue money are always rushed, always busy with urgent matters. Those who pursue the Dharma, go slow and easy. 'Boring', you say? Maybe. Maybe it's downright dreary to stop and smell a flower or listen to a bird. Maybe a glint of gold is really more dazzling than the sight of one's Original Face. Maybe what we need is a better definition of 'treasure'.

Han Shan, 1546–1623 (25)

If only men of every kind

Acted in accord with Buddha's words,

And kept back somewhat from their food
   for charity,

Then the result would be a great reward.

But whether at the first mouthful

Or at the last mouthful

If charity be not uppermost in the mind,

Then a man should not eat at all!

The Ngan-Shih-Niu Sutra, date unknown (27)

Once upon a time, I, Chuang, dreamt I was a
butterfly, fluttering hither and thither, to all
intents and purposes a butterfly. I was conscious
only of following my fancies as a butterfly, and
was unconscious of my individuality as a man.
Suddenly I awaked, and there I lay, myself again.
Now I do not know whether I was then a man
 dreaming I was a butterfly, or whether I am now

a butterfly dreaming I am a man. Between a man
and a butterfly there is necessarily a barrier. The
transition is called metempsychosis.

> Chuang Tzu, 4th century BCE (1)

道

All things that exist are transitory,

They must of necessity perish and
disappear,

Though joined together, there must be
separation,

Where there is life, there must be death,

All depends on conduct,

Whether good, or whether bad,

All things born,

Are unstable and inconstant.

The Ngan-Shih-Niu Sutra, date unknown (27)

What are the two most common goals for people who live in the world? Wealth and fame. To gain these goals people are willing to lose everything, including the health of their body, mind and spirit. Not a very good exchange, is it? Worldly wealth and fame fade so quickly that we wonder which will last longer, the money, the fame or the man. ...

But consider the goal of enlightenment, of attaining the wealth of the Dharma. Those who reach this goal are vigorous in body, keen in mind, and serene in spirit right into eternity.

Han Shan, 1546–1623 (25)

Getting and Wanting

No lure is greater than to posses what others want

No disaster greater than not to be content with what one has

No presage of evil greater than that men should be wanting to get more.

Lao Tzu, 6th century BCE (7)

Everyday Life is the Path

Joshu asked Nansen, 'What is the path?'

Nansen replied, 'Ordinary mind, that is, everyday life is the path.'

Joshu asked, 'Can I look for it?'

Nansen answered, 'If you try and find it, you will never know it.'

Joshu persisted. 'How can I find the path unless I look for it?'

Nansen said, 'The path is not a matter of knowing and not knowing. Knowing is delusion. Not knowing is confusion. When you really reach the true path, beyond doubt, you will find it as vast and boundless as outer space. How can it be talked about on the level of right and wrong?'

With these words, Joshu came to a sudden realisation.

Wu-men Hui-k'ai, 1183–216 (28)

— 3 —

ON HAPPINESS AND
THE ART OF LIVING

'Leave all things to take their natural
course, and do not interfere.'

Lao Tzu, 6th century BCE (29)

The Old Sweet, Peaceful Life

For ten long years I plodded through
the vale of lust and strife,

Then through my dreams there flashed a ray
of the old sweet peaceful life. ...

No scarlet-tasselled hat of state
can vie with soft repose;

[54]

Grand mansions do not taste the joys *amen!*
  that the poor man's cabin knows.

I hate the threatening clash of arms
  when fierce retainers throng,

I loathe the drunkard's revels and
  the sound of fife and song;

But I love to seek a quiet nook, *me too!*
  and some old volume bring

Where I can see the wild flowers bloom
  and hear the birds in spring.

Ch'en T'uan, d. 989 (21)

On Cherishing Life

Yen-Ping-Chung asked Kuan-Yi-Wu as to cherishing life.

Kuan-Yi-Wu replied, 'It suffices to give it its free course, neither checking nor obstructing it.'

Yen-Ping-Chung said: 'And as to details?'

Kuan-Yi-Wu replied: 'Allow the ear to hear what it likes, the eye to see what it likes, the nose to smell what it likes, the mouth to say what it likes, the body to enjoy the comforts it likes to have, and the mind to do what it likes.

'Now what the ear likes to hear is music, and the prohibition of it is what I call obstruction to the ear. What the eye likes to look at is beauty; and its not being permitted to regard this beauty I call obstruction of sight. What the nose likes to smell is perfume; and its not being permitted to smell I call obstruction to scent. What the mouth likes to talk about is right and wrong; and if it is not permitted to speak I call it obstruction of the understanding. The comforts the body enjoys to have are rich food and fine clothing; and if it is not permitted, then I call that obstruction of the senses of the body. What the mind likes is to be at peace; and its not being permitted rest I call obstruction of the mind's nature.

'All these obstructions are a source of the most painful vexation. Morbidly to cultivate this cause of vexation, unable to get rid of it, and so have a long but very sad life of a hundred, a thousand or ten thousand years, is not what I call cherishing life. But to check this source of obstruction and with calm enjoyment to await death for a day, a month, or a year or ten years, is what I understand by enjoying life.'

Yang Chu, c. 3rd century BCE (24)

The Joyous Life of Tuan-Mu-Shu

Tuan-Mu-Shu was descended from Tse-Kung. He had a patrimony of ten thousand gold pieces. Indifferent to the chances of life, he followed his own inclinations.

What the heart delights in, he would do and delight in; with his walls and buildings, pavilions, verandas, gardens, parks, ponds and lakes, wine and food, carriages, dresses, women and attendants, he would emulate the princes of Chi and Chu in luxury. Whenever his heart desired something, or his ear wished to hear something, his eye to see or his mouth to taste, he would procure it at all costs, though the thing might only be had in a far-off country, and not in the kingdom of Chi. When on a journey the mountains and rivers might be ever so difficult and dangerous to pass, and the roads ever so long, he would still proceed just as men walk a few steps.

A hundred guests were entertained daily in his palace. In the kitchens there were always fire and smoke, and the vaults of his hall and peristyle incessantly resounded with songs and music. The remains from his table he divided first among his clansmen. What they left was divided among his fellow-citizens, and what these did not eat was distributed throughout the whole kingdom.

When Tuan-Mu-Shu reached the age of sixty, and his mind and body began to decay, he gave up his household and distributed all his treasures, pearls and gems, carriages and dresses, concubines and female attendants. Within a year he had disposed of his fortune, and to his offspring he had left nothing. When he fell ill, he had no means to buy medicines and a stone lancet, and when he died, there was not even money for his funeral. All his countrymen who had benefited by him contributed money to bury him, and gave back the fortune of his descendants.

When Ch'in-ku-li heard of this he said, 'Tuan-Mu-Shu was a fool, who brought disgrace to his ancestors.'

When Tuan-Kan-Sheng heard of it he said, 'Tuan-Mu-Shu was a wise man; his virtue was much superior to that of his ancestors. The commonsense people were shocked at his conduct, but it was in accord with the right doctrine. The excellent man of Wei only adhered to propriety. They surely had not a heart like his.'

Yang Chu, c. 3rd century BCE (24)

The Two Big Humbugs

There is a wealth of humbug in this life, but the multitudinous little humbugs have been classified by Chinese Buddhists under two big humbugs: fame and wealth. Once a monk was discoursing with his pupil on these two sources of worldly cares, and said, 'It is easier to get rid of the desire for money than to get rid of the desire for fame. Even retired scholars and monks still want to be distinguished and well known among their company. They want to give public discourses to a large audience, and not to retire to a small monastery talking to one pupil, like you and me now.' The pupil replied, 'Indeed, Master, you are the only man in the world who has conquered the desire for fame!' And the Master smiled.

Lin Yutang, 1895–1976 (26)

Ah, Is This Not Happiness?

It is a hot day in June when the sun hangs still in the sky and there is not a whiff of wind or air … Suddenly there is a rumbling of thunder … Rain-water begins to pour down from the eaves like a cataract. The perspiration stops. The clamminess of the ground is gone. All flies disappear to hide themselves and I can eat my rice. Ah, is this not happiness?

To hear our children recite the classics so fluently, like the sound of pouring water from a vase. Ah, is this not happiness?

I get up early on a summer morning and see people sawing a large bamboo pole under a mat-shed, to be used as a water-pipe. Ah, is this not happiness?

It has been raining for a whole month and I lie in bed in the morning like one drunk or ill, refusing to get up. Suddenly I hear a chorus of birds announcing a clear day. Quickly I pull aside the curtain, push open the window and see the beautiful sun shining and glistening and the forest looks like having a bath. Ah, is this not happiness?

To cut with a sharp knife a bright-green watermelon on a big scarlet plate of summer afternoon. Ah, is this not happiness?

To find accidentally a handwritten letter from some old friend in a trunk. Ah, is this not happiness?

A traveller returns home after a long journey, and he sees the old city gate and hears the women and children on both banks of the river talking his own dialect. Ah, is this not happiness?

To watch someone writing big characters a foot high. Ah, is this not happiness?

To open the window to let the wasp out of the room. Ah, is this not happiness?

To see a wild prairie fire. Ah, is this not happiness?

To have just finished repaying all one's debts. Ah, is this not happiness?

Chin Shengt'an, 17th century CE (13)

The Happiness of a Fish

Chuang Tzu and Hui Tzu were taking a leisurely walk along the dam of the Hao River. Chuang Tzu said, 'The white fish are swimming at ease. This is the happiness of the fish.'

'You are not fish,' said Hui Tzu. 'How do you know its happiness?'

'You are not I,' said Chuang Tzu. 'How do you know that I do not know the happiness of the fish?'

Hui Tzu said, 'Of course I do not know, since I am not you. But you are not the fish, and it is perfectly clear that you do not know the happiness of the fish.'

'Let us get at the bottom of the matter,' said Chuang Tzu. 'When you asked how I knew the happiness of the fish, you already knew that I knew the happiness of the fish but asked how. I knew it along the river.'

Chuang Tzu, 4th century BCE (1)

Mixed Feelings

We scheme and fight with our minds. When we have small fears we are worried, and when we have great fears we are totally at a loss. One's mind shoots forth like an arrow to be the arbiter of right and wrong. Now it is reserved like a solemn pledge, in order to maintain its own advantage. Then, like the destruction of autumn and winter, it declines every day. Then it is sunk in pleasure and cannot be covered. Now it is closed like a seal; that is, it is old and exhausted. And finally it is near death and cannot be given life again. Pleasure and anger, sorrow and joy, anxiety and regret, fickleness and fear, impulsiveness and extravagance, indulgence and lewdness come to us like music from the hollows or like mushrooms from damp. Day and night they alternate within us but we know where they come from. Alas! These are with us morning and evening. It's here where they are produced! Without them [the feelings mentioned above] there would not be I. And without me who will experience them? They are right nearby. But we don't know who causes them. It seems there is a True Lord who does so, but there is no indication of his existence.

Chuang Tzu, 4th century BCE (1)

道

4

ON HOME, FAMILY AND FRIENDS

In the world, when a man and a woman mate they produce children, who eventually produce grandchildren, continuing from generation to generation. If there is a man without a woman, or a woman without a man, then solitary yin does not give birth, isolated yang does not promote growth – the productive mechanism stops.

What I realise as I observe this is the Tao of producing immortals and buddhas.

When people are first born, yin and yang are harmoniously combined and the spiritual embryo is perfectly complete. Then when they get involved in acquired temporal conditioning, yin and yang separate, and the spiritual embryo is damaged.

Liu I-Ming, 18th century CE (6)

The Loving Example
of One Family

From the loving example of one family a whole
state becomes loving, and from its courtesies the
whole state becomes courteous while, from the
ambition and perverseness of the One man, the
whole state may be led to rebellious disorder;
such is the nature of the influence. This verifies
the saying, 'Affairs may be ruined by a single
sentence; a kingdom may be settled by its One
man.' ...

'A happy union with wife and children is like
the music of lutes and harps! When there is
concord among brethren, the harmony is
delightful and enduring. Thus may you regulate
your family and enjoy the delights of wife and
children! The Master said, "In such a condition
parents find perfect contentment."'

Confucius, 551–479 BCE (30)

Homeward Bound I Go

Ah, homeward bound I go! Why not go home, seeing that my field and garden with weeds are overgrown? Myself have made my soul serf to my body: why have vain regrets and mourn alone?

Fret not over bygones and the forward journey take. Only a short distance have I gone astray, and I know today I am right, if yesterday was a complete mistake. ...

Then when I catch sight of my old roofs, joy will my steps quicken. Servants will be there to bid me welcome, and waiting at the door are the greeting children. ...

Ah, homeward bound I go! Let me from now on learn to live alone! The world and I are not made for one another, and why drive round like one looking for what he has not found?

There the trees, happy of heart, grow marvellously green, and spring water gushes forth with a gurgling sound. I admire how things grow and prosper according to their seasons, and feel that thus, too, shall my life go its round.

Enough! How long shall I this mortal shape

keep? Why not take life as it comes, and why hustle and bustle like one on an errand bound?

Wealth and power are not my ambitions, and unattainable is the abode of the gods! I would go forth alone on a bright morning, or perhaps, planting my cane, begin to pluck the weeds and till the ground.

Or I would compose a poem beside a clear stream, or perhaps go up Tungkao and make a long-drawn call on the top of the hill. So would I be content to live and die, and without questionings of the heart, gladly accept Heaven's will.

Yuänming, 365–427 (13)

Too Much Emotion …

'Twixt you and me

There's too much emotion.

That's the reason why

There's such a commotion!

Take a lump of clay,

Wet it, pat it,

And make an image of me,

And an image of you.

Then smash them, crash them,

And add a little water.

Break them and re-make them

Into an image of you,

And an image of me.

Then in my clay, there's a little of you.

And in your clay, there's a little me.

And nothing every shall us sever;

Living, we'll sleep in the same quilt,

And dead, we'll be buried together.

Madame Kuan, 1262–1319 (13)

道

Sharing With Friends

For enjoying flowers, one must secure big-hearted friends. For going to sing-song houses to have a look at sing-song girls, one must secure temperate friends. For going up a high mountain one must secure romantic friends. For boating, one must secure friends with an expansive nature. For facing the moon, one must secure friends with a cool philosophy. For anticipating snow, one must secure beautiful friends. For a wine party, one must secure friends with flavour and charm.

Anon. (13)

道

I have heard that it is in accordance with those rules (of propriety) that one should be chosen by others (as their model); I have not heard of his choosing them (to take him as such). I have heard in the same way of (scholars) coming to learn; I have not heard of (the master) going to teach. The course (of duty), virtue, benevolence, and right-eousness cannot be fully carried out without the rules of propriety; nor are training and oral lessons for the rectification of manners complete; nor can the clearing up of quarrels and discriminating in disputes be accomplished; nor can (the duties between) ruler and minister, high and low, father and son, elder brother and younger, be determined. ... Therefore the superior man is respectful and reverent, assiduous in his duties and not going beyond them, retiring and yielding; thus illustrating (the principle of) propriety.

The Lî Kî, c. 200 BCE (31)

道

In serving his father, (a son) should conceal (his faults), and not openly or strongly remonstrate with him about them; should in every possible way wait on and nourish him, without being tied to definite rules; should serve him laboriously till his death, and then complete the mourning for him for three years.

The Lî Kî, c. 200 BCE (32)

At the First Crowing of the Cock

Sons, in serving their parents, on the first crowing of the cock, should all wash their hands and rinse their mouths, (and) comb their hair ... Sons' wives should serve their parents-in-law as they served their own. At the first crowing of the cock, they should wash their hands, rinse their mouths and comb their hair. Thus dressed, they should go to their parents and parents-in-law. On getting to where they are, with bated breath and gentle voice, they should ask if their clothes are (too) warm or (too) cold, whether they are ill or pained, or uncomfortable in any part; and if they be so, they should proceed reverently to stroke and scratch the place. They should in the same way, going before or following after, help and support their parents in quitting or entering (the dwelling). In bringing in the basin for them to wash, the younger will carry the stand and the elder the water; they will beg to be allowed to pour out the water, and when the washing is concluded, they will hand the towel. They will ask whether they want anything, and then respectfully bring it. All this they will do with an appearance of pleasure to make their parents feel at ease. They should bring gruel, thick or thin, spirits or soup with vegetables, beans, wheat, spinach, rice, millet, maize, and glutinous millet, whatever they wish, in fact; with dates, chestnuts, sugar and honey, to sweeten their dishes; with the ordinary or the large-leaved violets, leaves of elm-trees, fresh or dry, and the most soothing rice-water to lubricate them; and with fat and oil to enrich them. The parents will be sure to taste them, and when they have done so, the young people should withdraw.

The Lî Kî, c. 200 BCE (33)

道

'Children and wife we love;

Union with them is sweet,

As lute's soft strain, that soothes our pain.

How joyous do we meet!

But brothers more than they

Can satisfy the heart.

'Tis their accord does peace afford,

And lasting joy impart.

For ordering of your homes,

For joy with child and wife,

Consider well the truth I tell;

This is the charm of life!'

The Lî Kî, c. 200 BCE (34)

道

The Ceremony of Marriage

The father gave himself the special cup to his son, and ordered him to go and meet the bride; it being proper that the male should take the first step (in all the arrangements). The son, having received the order, proceeded to meet his bride. Her father, who had been resting on his mat and leaning-stool in the temple, met him outside the gate and received him with a bow, and then the son-in-law entered, carrying a wild goose. After the (customary) bows and yieldings of precedence, they went up to the hall, when the bridegroom bowed twice and put down the wild goose. Then and in this way he received the bride from her parents.

After this they went down, and he went out and took the reins of the horses of her carriage, which he drove for three revolutions of the wheels, having handed the strap to assist her in mounting. He then went before, and waited outside his gate. When she arrived, he bowed to her as she entered. They ate together of the same animal, and joined in sipping from the cups made of the same melon. Thus showing that they now formed one body, were of equal rank, and pledged to mutual affection.

The respect, the caution, the importance, the attention to secure correctness in all the details, and then (the pledge of) mutual affection, these were the great points in the ceremony, and served to establish the distinction to be observed between man and woman, and the righteousness to be maintained between husband and wife. From the distinction between man and woman came the righteousness between husband and wife. From that righteousness came the affection between father and son; and from that affection, the rectitude between ruler and minister. Whence it is said, 'The ceremony of marriage is the root of the other ceremonial observances.'

The Lî Kî, c. 200 BCE (35)

Hexagram 37:
Chia Jen —The Family

THE TRIGRAMS

above: Sun – wind, gentleness, penetration
below: Li – fire, brightness, beauty

This hexagram represents the strength of the family. The strong yang line at the top represents the father, the strong bottom line, the son. The strong line in the fifth place may also represent the father, the weak yin line in the second place the wife; alternatively, the strong lines in the fifth and third place are two brothers, the weak second and fourth lines, their wives. Each individual line possesses the character in accordance with its position.

The Judgement: It is the woman's persistence that brings good fortune. Women who cast this hexagram should take it as a favourable omen, but for men it does not have a successful significance.

Commentary: It is the place of women to keep within; men stand without. Keeping to their appointed places, men and women act in accordance with the laws of heaven; when the family is in order, then all the social relationships of mankind are also in order. When father, mother, sons and brothers take their proper positions within the structure of the family, when husbands play their proper part and wives are truly wifely, all is well.

The Image: The wind rises from the fire. The words of the superior man are full of meaning, his life is constant and endures.

I Ching, written during the Zhou dynasty,
1122–256 BCE (11)

5

ON SOCIETY AND GOOD GOVERNMENT

A leader is best

When people barely know that he exists,

Not so good when people obey and
  acclaim him,

Worst when they despise him.

'Fail to honour people,

They fail to honour you.'

But of a good leader, who talks little,

When his work is done, his aim fulfilled,

They will all say, 'We did this ourselves.'

Lao Tzu, 6th century BCE (4)

The Master said, 'He who exercises government by means of his virtue may be compared to the north polar star, which keeps its place and all the stars turn towards it.'

Confucius, 551–479 BCE (14)

道

'When a country is well governed, poverty and a mean condition are things to be ashamed of. When a country is ill governed, riches and honour are things to be ashamed of.'

Confucius, 551–479 BCE (14)

道

Tsze-kung asked about government. The Master said, 'The requisites of government are that there be sufficiency of food, sufficiency of military equipment, and the confidence of the people in their ruler.'

Tsze-kung said, 'If it cannot be helped, and one of these must be dispensed with, which of the three should be foregone first?'

'The military equipment,' said the Master.

Tsze-kung again asked, 'If it cannot be helped, and one of the remaining two must be dispensed with, which of them should be foregone?'

The Master answered, 'Part with the food. From of old, death has been the lot of men; but if the people have no faith in their rulers, there is no standing for the state.'

Confucius, 551–479 BCE (14)

The Master said, 'When a prince's personal conduct is correct, his government is effective without the issuing of orders. If his personal conduct is not correct, he may issue orders, but they will not be followed.'

The Master said, 'If good men were to govern a country in succession for a hundred years, they would be able to transform the violently bad, and dispense with capital punishments.'

True indeed is this saying!

Confucius, 551–479 BCE (14)

Tsze-Chang asked about government. The Master said, 'The art of governing is to keep its affairs before the mind without weariness, and to practice them with undeviating consistency.'

Confucius, 551–479 BCE (14)

Tsze-Chang asked Confucius about government, saying, 'What do you say to killing the unprincipled for the good of the principled?' Confucius replied, 'Sir, in carrying on your government, why should you use killing at all? Let your evinced desires be for what is good, and the people will be good. The relation between superiors and inferiors is like that between the wind and the grass. The grass must bend, when the wind blows across it.'

Confucius, 551–479 BCE (14)

道

Tsze-lu asked about government. The Master said, 'Go before the people with your example, and be laborious in their affairs.'

He requested further instruction, and was answered, 'Be not weary in these things.'

Chung-kung, being chief minister to the head of the Chi family, asked about government. The Master said, 'Employ first the services of your various officers, pardon small faults, and raise to office men of virtue and talents.'

Chung-kung said, 'How shall I know the men of virtue and talent, so that I may raise them to office?' He was answered, 'Raise to office those whom you know. As to those whom you do not know, will others neglect them?'

Tsze-lu said, 'The ruler of Wei has been waiting for you, in order with you to administer the government. What will you consider the first thing to be done?'

The Master replied, 'What is necessary is to rectify names.'

'So! indeed!' said Tsze-lu. 'You are wide of the mark! Why must there be such rectification?'

The Master said, 'How uncultivated you are,

Yu! A superior man, in regard to what he does not know, shows a cautious reserve.

'If names be not correct, language is not in accordance with the truth of things. If language be not in accordance with the truth of things, affairs cannot be carried on to success.

'When affairs cannot be carried on to success, proprieties and music do not flourish. When proprieties and music do not flourish, punishments will not be properly awarded. When punishments are not properly awarded, the people do not know how to move hand or foot.

'Therefore a superior man considers it necessary that the names he uses may be spoken appropriately, and also that what he speaks may be carried out appropriately. What the superior man requires is just that in his words there may be nothing incorrect.'

Confucius, 551–479 BCE (14)

道

The Duke of Sheh Asks About Good Government

The Master said, 'Good government obtains when those who are near are made happy, and those who are far off are attracted.'

Tsze-hsia, being governor of Chu-fu, asked about government. The Master said, 'Do not be desirous to have things done quickly; do not look at small advantages. Desire to have things done quickly prevents their being done thoroughly. Looking at small advantages prevents great affairs from being accomplished.'

Confucius, 551–479 BCE (14)

The Right Conduct of a Person in Authority

Tsze-Chang asked Confucius, saying, 'In what way should a person in authority act in order that he may conduct government properly?'

The Master replied, 'Let him honour the five excellent, and banish away the four bad, things;

then may he conduct government properly.'

Tsze-Ch'ang said, 'What are meant by the five excellent things?'

The Master said, 'When the person in authority is beneficent without great expenditure; when he lays tasks on the people without their repining; when he pursues what he desires without being covetous; when he maintains a dignified ease without being proud; when he is majestic without being fierce.'

Tsze-Ch'ang said, 'What is meant by being beneficent without great expenditure?'

The Master replied, 'When the person in authority makes more beneficial to the people the things from which they naturally derive benefit, is not this being beneficent without great expenditure? When he chooses the labours which are proper, and makes them labour on them, who will repine? When his desires are set on benevolent government, and he secures it, who will accuse him of covetousness? Whether he has to do with many people or few, or with things great or small, he does not dare to indicate any disrespect; is not this to maintain a dignified ease without any pride? He adjusts his clothes and cap, and throws a dignity into his looks, so that, thus dignified, he is looked at with awe; is not this to be majestic without being fierce?'

Tsze-Ch'ang then asked, 'What are meant by the four bad things?'

The Master said, 'To put the people to death without having instructed them; this is called cruelty. To require from them, suddenly, the full tale of work, without having given them warning; this is called oppression. To issue orders as if without urgency, at first, and, when the time comes, to insist on them with severity; this is called injury. And, generally, in the giving of pay or rewards to men, to do it in a stingy way; this is called acting the part of a mere official.'

Confucius, 551–479 BCE (14)

The Right Government of the State

What is meant by 'In order rightly to govern the state, it is necessary first to regulate the family', is this: It is not possible for one to teach others, while he cannot teach his own family.

Therefore, the ruler, without going beyond his family, completes the lessons for the state. There is filial piety: therewith the Sovereign should be served. There is fraternal submission: therewith elders and superiors should be served. There is kindness: therewith the multitude should be treated.

Confucius, 551–479 BCE (14)

Making the Kingdom Peaceful and Happy

What is meant by 'Making the whole kingdom peaceful and happy depends on the government of his state'? When the sovereign behaves to his aged, as the aged should be behaved to, the people become final; when the sovereign behaves to his elders, as the elders should be behaved to, the people learn brotherly submission; when the sovereign treats compassionately the young and helpless, the people do the same. Thus, the ruler has a principle with which, as with a measuring square, he may regulate his conduct. What a man dislikes in his superiors, let him not display in the treatment of his inferiors; what he dislikes in inferiors, let him not display in the service of his superiors.

This is what is called 'The principle with which, as with a measuring square, to regulate one's conduct.'

Confucius, 551–479 BCE (14)

道

Governing a great state is like cooking a small fish.

Lao Tzu, 6th century BCE (7)

The Great Principle

'When the Great Principle (of the Great Similarity) prevails, the whole world becomes a republic; they elect men of talents, virtue, and ability; they talk about sincere agreement, and cultivate universal peace. Thus men do not regard as their parents only their own parents, nor treat as their children only their own children.

A competent provision is secured for the aged till their death, employment for the middle-aged, and the means of growing up for the young. The widowers, widows, orphans, childless men, and those who are disabled by disease, are all sufficiently maintained. Each man has his rights, and each woman her individuality safeguarded. They produce wealth, disliking that it should be thrown away upon the ground, but not wishing to keep it for their own gratification. Disliking idleness, they labour, but not alone with a view to their own advantage. In this way selfish schemings are repressed and find no way to arise. Robbers, filchers and rebellious traitors do not exist.

Hence the outer doors remain open, and are not shut. This is the state of what I call the Great Similarity.'

Confucius, 551–479 BCE (36)

The World at Peace: the first lesson of Sung Dynasty school curriculum

The ancient people who desired to have a clear moral harmony in the world would first order their national life; those who desired to order their national life would first regulate their home life; those who desired to regulate their home life would first cultivate their personal lives; those who desired to cultivate their personal lives would first set their hearts right; those who desired to set their hearts right would first make their will sincere; those who desired to make their wills sincere would first arrive at understanding; understanding comes from the exploration of knowledge of things. When knowledge of things is gained, then understanding is reached; when understanding is reached, then the will is sincere; when the will is sincere, then the heart is set right; when the heart is set right, then the personal life is cultivated; when the personal life is cultivated, then the home life is regulated; when the home life is regulated, then national life is orderly; and when national life is orderly, then the world is at peace.

There is a cause and a sequence in things, and a beginning and end in human affairs. To know the order and precedence is to have the beginning of wisdom.

Lin Yutang, 1895–1976 (26)

道

Not to consider right the rules laid down by one's teacher, but to prefer one's own ways, is as if a blind man were to try to distinguish colours, or a deaf man to distinguish sounds; there is no way to avoid confusion and error.

Chuang Tzu, 4th century BCE (1)

The Meaning of the Ceremony of Archery

Therefore, anciently, the son of Heaven chose the feudal lords, the dignitaries who were Great officers, and the officers, from their skill in archery. Archery is specially the business of males, and there were added to it the embellishments of ceremonies and music. Hence among the things which may afford the most complete illustration of ceremonies and music, and the frequent performance of which may serve to establish virtue and good conduct, there is nothing equal to archery: and therefore the ancient kings paid much attention to it.

Therefore, anciently, according to the royal institutes, the feudal princes annually presented the officers who had charge of their tribute to the son of Heaven, who made trial of them in the archery-hall. Those of them whose bodily carriage was in conformity with the rules, and whose shooting was in agreement with the music, and who hit the mark most frequently, were allowed to take part at the sacrifices. When his officers had frequently that privilege, their ruler was congratulated; if they frequently failed to obtain it, he was reprimanded. If a prince were frequently so congratulated, he received an increase to his territory; if he were frequently so reprimanded, part of his territory was taken from him. Hence came the saying, 'The archers shoot in the interest of their princes'. Thus, in the states, the rulers and their officers devoted themselves to archery, and the practice in connexion with it of the ceremonies and music. But when rulers and officers practise ceremonies and music, never has it been known that such practice led to their banishment or ruin.

The Lî Kî, c. 200 BCE (37)

Stop killing!

For countless years the bitter stew of hate
goes boiling on.

Its vengeful broth is ocean deep,
impossible to calm.

To learn the cause of all this conflict,

Terror, bombs and war,

Listen to the cries at midnight by the
butcher's door.

Ch'an Master Cloud of Vows, Song Dynasty,
960–1279 (19)

道

Hexagram 34:
Ta Chuang – the Strength of Greatness

THE TRIGRAMS

above: Chen – Thunder and awakening

below: Ch'ien – Heaven, the creative

The four strong yang lines have entered from below and are ascending; the combination of the strength of Ch'ien with the powerful movement of Chen is what gives meaning to this hexagram. In appearance, it is reminiscent of the horned head of the goat, an animal renowned for rapid, powerful movement. The hexagram is also linked with the second month of the Chinese year, the time when everything is springing strongly into life.

The Judgement: Ta Chuang is the strength of the great. Perseverance in a course of righteousness brings reward.

Commentary: The strength of righteousness and greatness combine to bring full understanding of the inner nature of everything in heaven and on earth. The lower trigram, signifying strength, controls the upper, which signifies movement, and from this results great vigour. Righteous persistence is duly rewarded because, in the context of this hexagram, what is great and what is right are synonymous.

The Image: Thunder above the heavens is the image of the strength of greatness. The superior man does not lead a path that is not in accord with the established order.

I Ching, written during the Zhou dynasty, 1122–256 BCE (11)

6

ON THE USE AND ENJOYMENT OF NATURE

Green creek – the water from the source
  is limpid.

Cold Mountain – the halo of the moon
  is white.

Silent illumination, the mind is realized
  by itself.

Knowing the void, delusion turns into
  tranquillity.

Han Shan, c. 8th century CE (38)

Plants and trees first flower and then produce fruit, each in its season. This is why they can live a long time. If they miss their season, this is a fore-sign of death, because it is abnormal.

What I realise as I observe this is the Tao of going along with time.

What human life depends on is spirit and energy. Therefore wise people are as careful of their vitality and spirit as one would be of jewels.

Liu I-Ming, 18th century CE (6)

道

The stem of the lotus is hollow, so on emerging from the mud it is extraordinarily clean. The flower of the chrysanthemum is late, so on meeting the autumn frost it is extraordinarily fresh. When the inside is hollow, then outside things cannot leave their mark; when the flower is late, the energy is full and resistant to cold.

What I realise as I observe this is the Tao of cultivating the inward and being immune to externals.

Liu I-Ming, 18th century CE (6)

Hibernation

At the end of autumn, insects go into hibernation. In the spring, they return to life. Their rebirth is based on their hibernation.

What I realise as I observe this is the Tao of finding life in the midst of death.

The reason people do not attain lasting life is that they are unable to die first. To die means to make the human mentality die, to live means to make the mind of Tao live. … If you want to give life to the mind of Tao, you must first cause the human mentality to die.

Liu I-Ming, 18th century CE (6)

道

Everything that exists on earth is but the transient form of appearance of some celestial agency. Everything terrestrial has its prototype, its primordial cause, its ruling agency in heaven. The Chinese philosopher, looking at the beauties of nature, the variety of hills and plains, rivers and oceans, the wonderful harmony of colour, light and shade, sees in it but the dim reflex of that more splendid scenery frescoed in ethereal beauty on heaven's starry firmament. He gazes at the sun, that dazzling regent of the day, and recognizes in him, as his terrestrial reflex, the male principle of creation, ruling everything that is under the sun. He lifts up his eye to the moon, the beautiful queen of the night, and sees her reflex on earth, in the female principle, pervading all sublunary forms of existence. He observes the swift rotatory course of the five planets, Jupiter, Mars, Venus, Mercury and Saturn, and sees their counterpart on earth in the ceaseless interchange and permutations of the five elements of nature, wood, fire, metal, water and earth. He contemplates the spangled firmament at night, and compares with it its dimly reflected transcript on the surface of our earth, where the mountain peaks form the stars, the rivers and oceans answer to the milky way.

The Feng Shui, 19th century CE (39)

Returning to Live in the Country 1

Young, I was always free of common feeling.

It was in my nature to love the hills and
mountains.

Mindlessly I was caught in the dust-filled
trap.

Waking up, thirty years had gone.

The caged bird wants the old trees and air.

Fish in their pool miss the ancient stream.

I plough the earth at the edge of South Moor.

Keeping life simple, return to my plot and
garden.

My place is hardly more than a few fields.

My house has eight or nine small rooms.

Elm-trees and Willows shade the back.

Plum-trees and Peach-trees reach the door.

Misted, misted the distant village.

Drifting, the soft swirls of smoke.

Somewhere a dog barks deep in the winding
lanes.

A cockerel crows from the top of the mulberry
tree.

No heat and dust behind my closed doors.

My bare rooms are filled with space and
silence.

Too long a prisoner, captive in a cage,

Now I can get back again to Nature.

T'ao Ch'ien, 365–427 (16)

Thoughts of Home

I awake, and moonbeams play around my bed,

Glittering like hoar-frost to my wondering eyes;

Up towards the glorious moon I raise my head,

Then lay me down – and thoughts of home
arise.

Li Po, 705–62 (21)

There was once a time when the forests of Niu Mountain were beautiful. But can the mountain any longer be regarded as beautiful, since being situated near a big city, the woodsmen have hewed the trees down? The days and nights gave it rest, and the rains and the dew continued to nourish it, and a new life was continually springing up from the soil, but then the cattle and the sheep began to pasture on it. That is why the Niu Mountain looks so bald, and when people see its baldness, they imagine that there never was timber on the mountain. Is this the true nature of the mountain? And is there not a heart of love and righteousness in man, too? But how can that nature remain beautiful when it is hacked down every day, as the woodsman chops down the trees with his axe? To be sure, the nights and days do the healing and there is the nourishing air of the early dawn, which tends to keep him sound and normal, but this morning air is thin and is soon destroyed by what he does in the day. With this continuing hacking of the human spirit, the rest and recuperation obtained during the night are not sufficient to maintain its level, and when

and today!

the night's recuperation does not suffice to maintain its level, then the man degrades himself to a state not far from a beast's. People see that he acts like a beast and imagine that there was never any true character in him. But is this the true nature of man?

Mencius, 372–289 BCE (17)

道

The mountain trees plunder themselves, the grease over a fire fries itself. Cinnamon can be eaten, therefore the trees that yield it are chopped down. Varnish can be used, therefore the trees that produce it are hacked. Everyone knows the utility of usefulness, but nobody knows the utility of uselessness.

Chuang Tzu, 4th century BCE (40)

道

Sow the seed widely among the sentient beings,

And it will come to fruition on fertile ground.

Without sentience no seed can grow;

Nor can there be life without nature.

Ma-tzu Tao-I, 709–88 (41)

道

It was the time of autumn floods. Every stream poured into the river, which swelled in its turbid course. The banks receded so far from each other that it was impossible to tell a cow from a horse.

Then the Spirit of the River laughed for joy that all the beauty of the earth was gathered to himself. Down with the stream he journeyed east until he reached the ocean. There, looking eastwards and seeing no limit to its waves, his countenance changed. And as he gazed over the expanse, he sighed and said to the Spirit of the Ocean, 'A vulgar proverb says that he who has heard but part of the truth thinks no one equal to himself. And such a one am I.

'When formerly I heard people detracting from

the learning of Confucius or underrating the heroism of Poh I, I did not believe. But now that I have looked upon your inexhaustibility – alas for me had I not reached your abode, I should have been for ever a laughing-stock to those of comprehensive enlightenment!'

To which the Spirit of the Ocean replied: 'You cannot speak of ocean to a well-frog – the creature of a narrower sphere. You cannot speak of ice to a summer insect – the creature of a season. You cannot speak of Tao to a pedagogue: his scope is too restricted. But now that you have emerged from your narrow sphere and have seen the great ocean, you know your own insignificance, and I can speak to you of great principles …

Chuang Tzu, 4th century BCE (1)

道

He who knows the activities of Nature and the activities of man is perfect. He who knows the activities of Nature lives according to Nature. He who knows the activities of man nourishes what he does not know with what he does know, thus completing his natural span of life and will not die prematurely half of the way. This is knowledge at its supreme greatness.

However, there is a defect here. For knowledge depends on something to be correct, but what it depends on is uncertain and changeable. How do we know that what I call Nature is not really man and what I call man is not really Nature?

Chuang Tzu, 4th century BCE (1)

道

In spring flowers, the autumn the harvest
   moon;

Summer breezes, in winter snow.

If useless things do not clutter your mind,

Any season is a good season for you.

Wu-men Hui-k'ai, 1183–216 (28)

7

ON THE WAY

To talk about food does not fill your belly,

To talk about clothes does not keep you warm.

To satisfy your hunger you must have a meal,

To escape the cold you must have clothes
to wear.

But you cannot detach from pondering and
scrutinizing,

And from asserting that to follow Buddha is
impossible.

Turn your gaze into your heart and at once you
are Buddha –

You will never find him outside of yourself!

Han Shan, c. 8th century CE (38)

There is nothing to be taught, nothing to be transmitted. It is just a matter of seeing one's own nature.

Dajian Huineng, 638–713 (42)

道

Abide in stillness and you will gradually enter the true way. When you enter the true way, this is called receiving the Tao.

Lao Tzu, 6th century BCE (7)

道

'So!' said the Old Master, 'If the Way could be presented, then everyone would present it to his lord. If the Way could be offered, then everybody would offer it to his parents. If the Way could be told, then everyone would tell it to his brothers. If the Way could be given, then everybody would give it to his descendants.'

Chuang Tzu, 4th century BCE (40)

The great Way is ineffable, great disputation is speechless, great humaneness is inhumane, great honesty is immodest and great bravery is not aggressive. The way that displays itself is not the Way. Speech that is disputatious fails to achieve its aims. Humaneness that is constant cannot go around. Honesty that is aloof will not be trusted. Bravery that is aggressive will not succeed. One who does not abandon these five precepts will be more or less headed in the right direction.

Therefore she who knows to stop at what she does not know has attained the ultimate. Who knows the disputation that is without words and the Way that cannot be walked upon? If one can have knowledge of them, this is called the Treasury of Heaven. You may pour into it, but it never fills; you may dip from it, but it never empties; and you never know where it comes from. This is called the Inner Light.

Chuang Tzu, 4th century BCE (40)

A thousand lives, ten thousand deaths

How long shall this keep going on?

Being born and dying, coming and going –

From defilement to darkness deep,

They do not see within their own hearts,

The priceless jewel they own –

Still they are like a blind donkey

Obediently trotting along.

Han Shan, c. 8th century CE (38)

The Original Real Human

The Tao connects with the spiritual. Once understood, it applies to everything, going beyond the dust of the ordinary world. Recognize the original formless thing, and forge it into an adamantine, indestructible body. This is most sacred, most spiritual – the three poisons of greed, aggression and stupidity die out, there are no calamities, no difficulties, all seasons are spring. This method has no difficulty, it is really simple and easy; nevertheless, in this world there are few real people.

Liu I-Ming, 18th century CE (6)

Preserving Spirit

The firing is the spirit. Vitality cannot be concentrated except by energy, but vitality and energy cannot be operated without the spirit to stabilise the vitality, and nurturing the energy is just a matter of preserving the spirit. In the work of preserving the spirit, it is important to stop rumination, with nothing coming out from within and nothing coming in from outside. With all signs of emotion gone, one plunges into a state of boundlessness, lightness, blissful fluidity, tranquil independence.

Ancestor Lü, 8th century CE (43)

Only the Tao is Natural

The Tao is natural. All forced manipulation and concoctions are in vain. Some people guard their minds and settle their ideas and thoughts, some people hold their breath and keep it in the abdomen, some people perform psychosomatic energy-circulation exercises. When these people come to the end of their lives and find everything they did was useless, they will resent the gods, also uselessly.

Liu I-Ming, 18th century CE (6)

The Essential Breath

Men are all possessed of Essential Vigour; this corresponds with the Spirit, the Spirit with the Breath, and the Breath with the essential nature of the body. Those who have not obtained their original or essential nature, all usurp their reputation.

The Spirit is able to enter stone; the Spirit is able to fly through solid bodies. If it enters water, it is not drowned; or fire, it is not burned. The Spirit depends, for its birth, upon the body; the Essential Vigour depends, for attaining its full proportions, upon the Breath. They never lose their vitality or force, but are evergreen, like the pine and cedar trees. The three are all one Principle. Their mystery and beauty cannot be heard. The combination of them produces existence; their dispersion, extinction.

The Hsin Yin Ching, date unknown (44)

The Tao is a Treasure

The Tao is a treasure. If you understand it, it can extend your life span. This has nothing to do with material alchemy. It is utterly simple, utterly easy, there is no difficulty involved. It is completely spiritual, true goodness. The ridiculous thing is that foolish people seek mysterious marvels, when they do not know enough to preserve the mysterious marvel that is actually present. *Amen!*

Liu I-Ming, 18th century CE (6)

The Roads Leading to the Tao

There are many roads leading to the Tao, but essentially they fall into two categories. The one is 'Entrance by way of Reason' and the other 'Entrance by way of Conduct'.

By 'Entrance by way of Reason' we mean the understanding of the fundamental doctrines through the study of the scriptures, the realization, upon the basis of a deep-rooted faith, that all sentient beings have in common the one True Nature, which does not manifest itself clearly in all cases only because it is over-wrapped by external objects and false thoughts. If a man abandons the false and returns to the true, resting single-heartedly and without distraction in pure contemplation, he will realize that there is neither self nor other, that the holy and profane are of one essence. If he holds on firmly to this belief and never swerves from it, he will never again be a slave to the letter of the scriptures, being in secret communion with Reason itself and altogether emancipated from conceptual discrimination. In this way, he will enjoy perfect serenity and spontaneity. This is called 'Entrance by way of Reason'.

'Entrance by way of Conduct' refers to the four rules of conduct under which all other rules can be subsumed. They are (1) the rule of requital of hatred, (2) the rule of adaptation to variable conditions and circumstances of life, (3) the rule of non-attachment, and (4) the rule of acting in accord with the Dharma.

THE REQUITAL OF HATRED

When a pursuer of the Tao falls into any kind of suffering and trials, he should think and say to himself thus: 'During the innumerable past kalpas I have abandoned the essential and followed after the accidentals, carried along on the restless waves of the sea of existences, and thereby creating endless occasions for hate, ill-will and wrong-doing. Although my present suffering is not caused by any offences committed in this life, yet it is a fruit of my sins in my past existences, which happens to ripen at this moment. It is not something which any men or gods could have given to me. Let me therefore take, patiently and sweetly, this bitter fruit of my own making without resentment or complaint against anyone.' The Scripture teaches us not to be disturbed by painful experiences. Why? Because of a penetrating insight into the real cause of all our sufferings. When this mind is awakened in a man, it responds spontaneously to the dictates of Reason, so that it can even help him to make the best use of other people's hatred and turn it into an occasion of advance toward the Tao. This is called the 'rule of requital of hatred'.

THE RULE OF ADAPTATION

We should know that all sentient beings are produced by the interplay of karmic conditions, and as such there can be no real self in them. The mingled yarns of pleasure and pain are all woven of the threads of conditioning causes. If therefore I should be rewarded with fortune, honour and other pleasant things, I must realize that they are the effects of my previous deeds destined to be reaped in this life. But as soon as their conditioning causes are exhausted, they will vanish away. Then why should I be elated over them?

Therefore, let gains and losses run their natural courses according to the ever-changing conditions and circumstances of life, for the Mind itself does not increase with the gains nor decrease with the losses. In this way, no gales of self-complacency will arise, and your mind will remain in hidden harmony with the Tao. It is in this sense that we must understand 'the rule of adaptation to the variable conditions and circumstances of life'.

THE RULE OF NON-ATTACHMENT

Men of the world remain unawakened for life; everywhere we find them bound by their craving and clinging. This is called 'attachment'. The wise however understand the truth, and their reason tells them to turn from the worldly ways. They enjoy peace of mind and perfect detachment. They adjust their bodily movements to the vicissitudes of fortune, always aware of the emptiness of the phenomenal world, in which they find nothing to delight in. Merit and demerit are ever interpenetrated, like light and darkness. To stay too long in the triple world is to live in a house on fire. Everyone who has a body is an heir to suffering and a stranger to peace. Having comprehended this point, the wise are detached from all things of the phenomenal world, with their minds free of desires and craving. As the Scripture has it, 'All sufferings spring from attachment; true joy arises from detachment.' To know clearly the bliss of detachment is to walk on the path of the Tao. This is 'the rule of non-attachment'.

THE RULE OF ACTING IN ACCORD WITH THE DHARMA

Dharma is nothing else than Reason which is pure in its essence. This pure Reason is the formless Form of all Forms; it is free of all defilements and attachments, and it knows of neither 'self' nor 'other'. As the Scripture says, 'In the Dharma there are no sentient beings, that is, it is free from the stain of sentient beings. In the Dharma there is no self, that is, it is free from the stain of the self.' When the wise are convinced of this truth, they should live in harmony with the Dharma.

Bodhidharma, 5th century BCE (41)

The Great Way

The Great Way is very difficult to express in words. Because it is hard to speak of, just look into beginninglessness, the beginningless beginning. When you reach the point where there is not even any beginninglessness, and not even any non-existence of beginninglessness, this is the primordial. The primordial Way cannot be assessed; there is nothing in it that can be assessed. What verbal explanation is there for it? We cannot explain it, yet we do explain it — where does the explanation come from? The Way that can be explained is only in doing. What is doing? It is attained by nondoing. This nondoing begins in doing.

Ancestor Lü, 8th century CE (43)

Real Constancy

This Tao is the Way of real constancy and true eternity. It is easy to get confused by things when dealing with situations, so when you come in contact with people, it will not do to get confused by what happens.

If you do not respond to people, then you are empty and silent, an open absence; when they come to you, you ought to respond, then let the thing pass when it's past. Be clear, upright, and magnanimous, and you won't be confused. Your true nature will then be clear and serene, while your original spirit will solidify and crystallize.

Ch'ang San-Feng, various suggested dates between 1247 and 1464 (45)

Clarifying the Way

The Tao is always to be practiced in the midst of daily life. Stop talking about lofty wonders and the empty void. Just carry out the human Tao and there will be no shame in your heart. When you fulfil your nature, you'll know heaven and earth are the same.

Wang Wei-I, c. 1323–c. 1374 (46)

The Half-and-Half Song

By far the greater half have I seen through

This floating life – ah, there's a magic word –

This 'half' – so rich in implications.

It bids us taste of joy of more than we

Can ever own. Half-way in life is man's

Best estate, when slackened pace allows him
   ease;

A wide world lies half-way 'twixt heaven
   and earth;

To live half-way between the town and the
   land,

Have farms half-way between the streams
   and hills;

Be half-a-scholar, and half-a-squire, and half

In business; half as gentry live,

And half related to the common folk;

And have a house that's half genteel, half plain,

Half elegantly furnished and half bare;

Dresses and gowns that are half old, half new,

And food half epicure's, half simple fare;

Have servants not too clever, not too dull;

A wife who's not too simple, nor too smart –

So then, at heart, I feel I'm half a Buddha,

And almost half a Taoist fairy blest.

One half myself to Father Heave I

Return; the other half to children leave –

Half thinking how for my posterity

To plan and provide, and yet half minding how

To answer god when the body's laid at rest.

He is most wisely drunk who is half drunk;

And flowers in half-bloom look their prettiest;

As boats at half-sail sail the steadiest,

And horses held at half-slack reins trot best.

Who half too much has, adds anxiety,

But half too little, adds possession's zest.

Since life's of sweet and bitter compounded,

Who tastes but half is wise and cleverest.

Li Mi-an, 717–86 (13)

道

Life follows upon death. Death is the beginning
of life. Who knows when the end is reached? The
life of man results from convergence of the vital
fluid. Its convergence is life; its dispersion, death.
If, then, life and death are but consecutive states,
what need have I to complain? Therefore all
things are One. What we love is animation. What
we hate is corruption. But corruption in its turn
becomes animation, and animation once more
becomes corruption.

The universe is very beautiful, yet it says
nothing. The four seasons abide by a fixed law,
yet they are not heard. All creation is based upon
absolute principles, yet nothing speaks.

And the true Sage, taking his stand upon the
beauty of the universe, pierces the principles of
created things. Hence the saying that the perfect

man does nothing, the true Sage performs nothing, beyond gazing at the universe. For man's intellect, however keen, face to face with the countless evolutions of things, their death and birth, their squareness and roundness, can never reach the root. There creation is, and there it has ever been.

Chuang Tzu, 4th century BCE (1)

道

What is God-given is called nature; to follow nature is called Tao, the Way; to cultivate the Way is called culture. Before joy, anger, sadness and happiness are expressed, they are called the inner self; when they are expressed to the proper degree, they are called harmony. The inner self is the correct foundation of the world, and harmony is the illustrious Way. When a man has achieved the inner self and harmony, the heaven and earth are orderly and the myriad of things are nourished and grow thereby.

Tsesse (grandson of Confucius), 492–431 BCE (13)

Experience Ch'an

1 Experience Ch'an! It's not mysterious.

As I see it, it boils down to cause and effect.

Outside the mind there is no Dharma

So how can anybody speak of a heaven beyond?

2 Experience Ch'an! It's not a field of learning.

Learning adds things that can be researched and discussed.

The feel of impressions can't be communicated.

Enlightenment is the only medium of transmission.

3 Experience Ch'an! It's not a lot of questions.

Too many questions is the Ch'an disease.

The best way is just to observe the noise of the world.

The answer to your questions?

Ask your own heart.

4 Experience Ch'an! It's not the teachings
  of disciples.

  Such speakers are guests from outside the
    gate.

  The Ch'an which you are hankering to speak
    about

  Only talks about turtles turning into fish.

5 Experience Ch'an! It can't be described.

  When you describe it you miss the point.

  When you discover that your proofs are
    without substance

  You'll realize that words are nothing
    but dust.

6 Experience Ch'an! It's experiencing your
  own nature!

Going with the flow everywhere and always.

When you don't fake it and waste time trying
  to rub and polish it,

Your Original Self will always shine through
  brighter than bright.

7 Experience Ch'an! It's like harvesting
  treasures.

But donate them to others.

You won't need them.

Suddenly everything will appear before you,

Altogether complete and altogether done.

8 Experience Ch'an! Become a follower who
  when accepted

Learns how to give up his life and his death.

Grasping this carefully he comes to see clearly.

And then he laughs till he topples the Cold
Mountain ascetics.

9 Experience Ch'an! It'll require great
scepticism;

But great scepticism blocks those detours on
the road.

Jump off the lofty peaks of mystery.

Turn your heaven and earth inside out.

10 Experience Ch'an! Ignore that superstitious
nonsense

That makes some claim that they've attained
Ch'an.

Foolish beliefs are those of the not-yet-
awakened.

And they're the ones who most need the
experience of Ch'an!

11 Experience Ch'an! There's neither distance
    nor intimacy.

Observation is like a family treasure.

Whether with eyes, ears, body, nose, or
    tongue —

It's hard to say which is the most amazing
    to use.

12 Experience Ch'an! There's no class
    distinction.

The one who bows and the one who is bowed
    to are a Buddha unit.

The yoke and its lash are tied to each other.

Isn't this our first principle ... the one we
    should most observe?

Hsu Yun, 1840–1959 (47)

道

Life has its distinctions; but in death we are all made equal. That death should have an origin, but that life should have no origin – can this be so? What determines its presence in one place, its absence in another? Heaven has its fixed order. Earth has yielded up its secrets to man. But where to seek whence am I?

Not knowing the hereafter, how can we deny the operation of Destiny? Not knowing what preceded birth, how can we assert the operation of Destiny? When things turn out as they ought, who shall say that the agency is not supernatural? When things turn out otherwise, who shall say that it is?

Chuang Tzu, 4th century BCE (1)

道

Being and Not-Being

It is because every one under Heaven recognizes beauty as beauty, that the idea of ugliness exists.

And equally if every one recognized virtue as virtue, this would merely create fresh conceptions of wickedness.

For truly, Being and Not-being grow out of one another;

Difficult and easy complete one another.

Long and short test one another;

High and low determine one another.

Pitch and mode give harmony to one another.

Front and back give sequence to one another.

Therefore the Sage relies on actionless activity,

Carries on wordless teaching,

But the myriad creatures are worked upon by him; he does not disown them.

He rears them, but does not lay claim to them,

Controls them, but does not lean upon them,

Achieves his aim, but does not call attention to
what he does;

And for the very reason that he does not call
attention to what he does

He is not ejected from fruition of what he has
done.

Lao Tzu, 6th century BCE (7)

A Story

Some time during the reign of Chen-kuan
(627–50), Tao-hsin, the fourth Patriarch of the
Chinese School of Ch'an, looking at the Niu-t'ou
Mountain from afar, was struck by its ethereal
aura, indicating that there must be some extra-
ordinary man living there. So he took it upon
himself to come to look for the man. When he
arrived at the temple, he asked a monk, 'Is there
a man of Tao around here?'

The monk replied, 'Who among the home-
leavers are not men of Tao?'

Tao-hsin said, 'But which of you is the man of Tao, after all?'

Another monk said, 'About three miles from here, there is a man who people call the Lazy Yung, because he never stands up when he sees anybody, nor gives any greeting. Can he be the man of Tao you are looking for?'

Tao-hsin then went deeper into the mountain and found Niu-t'ou sitting quietly and paying no attention to him. Tao-hsin approached him, asking, 'What are you doing here?'

'Contemplating the mind,' said Niu-t'ou.

'But who is contemplating, and what is the mind contemplated?' Tao-hsin asked.

Stunned by the question, Niu-t'ou rose from his seat and greeted him courteously, saying, 'Where does Your Reverence live?'

'My humble self has no definite place to rest in, roving east and west.'

'Do you happen to know the Ch'an master Tao-hsin?'

'Why do you ask about him?'

'I have looked up to him for long, hoping to pay my homage to him some day.'

'This humble monk is none other than Tao-hsin.'

'What has moved you to condescend to come to this place?'

'For no other purpose than to visit you!'

Tao-hsin went on to say: 'There are hundreds and thousands of dharmas and yogas, but all of them have their home in the heart. ... All operations of cause and effect are like dreams and illusion. Actually there are no three realms to escape from. Nor is there any Bodhi or enlightenment to seek after. All beings, human and non-human, belong to one universal, undifferentiated Nature. Great Tao is perfectly empty and free of all barriers; it defies all thought and meditation. ... All that you need is to let the mind function and rest in its perfect spontaneity. Do not set it upon contemplation or action, nor try to purify it. Without craving, without anger, without sorrow or care, let the mind move in untrammelled freedom, going where it pleases ...'

Nan-yueh Huai-jang, 677–744 (41)

Within and Without

The Buddha, The Reverend One of the World,

ascended the Snowy Peak.

Whoever witnessed this?

Relying on the heartlessness of my sword

I went and cut off all my black hair.

Whatever the style, a surface appearance is
   essentially just that –

the outside of something.

Whatever the determination, a plan to perform
   any Dharma method isessentially just that –

an interior scheme.

Only the person who gets rid of within and
   without

Escapes from birth and death and ascends to
   eternity.

Hsu Yun, 1840–1959 (47)

Joshu's Dog

A monk asked Joshu, 'Has a dog the Buddha Nature?'

Joshu answered, 'Mu.'

Mumon's Comment:

In order to master Ch'an, you must pass the barrier of the patriarchs. To attain this subtle realisation you must completely cut off the way of thinking. If you do not pass the barrier, and do not cut off the way of thinking, then you will be like a ghost clinging to the bushes and weeds. Now, I want to ask you, what is this barrier of the patriarchs? Why, it is this single word, 'Mu'. That is the front gate to Ch'an. ...

If you want to pass this barrier you must work through every bone in your body, through every pore in you skin, filled with this question, 'What is Mu?' and carry it day and night. Do not believe it is the common negative symbol meaning, nothing. It is not nothingness, the opposite of existence. ...

Just concentrate your whole energy into this Mu, and do not stop even for a passing moment.

Employ every ounce of energy to work on this 'Mu', and if you do this without interruption you will light a candle that will illuminate the whole universe.

Has a dog Buddha nature?

This is the most serious question of all.

If you say yes or no,

You lose your own Buddha-nature.

Wu-men Hui-k'ai, 1183–260 (28)

道

8

ON THE MIND
AND ITS RIGHT USE

Question: 'Since there is nothing on which to lay hold, how should the Dharma be transmitted?'

Answer: 'It is transmitted from mind to mind.'

Question: 'If mind is used for this purpose, how can it be said that mind does not exist?'

Answer: 'Obtaining absolutely nothing is called receiving transmission from mind to mind.'

Question: 'If there is no mind and no Dharma, what is meant by "transmission"?'

Answer: 'It is because you people on hearing of transmission from mind to mind, take it to mean that there is something to be obtained, that Bodhidharma said:

"The nature of the mind, when understood,

No human word can compass or disclose.

Enlightenment is naught to be obtained,

And he that gains it does not say he knows."

If I were to make this clear to you, I doubt you
could stand up to such knowledge.'

Hsi Yun, 9th century CE (48)

The Checkpoint

The Gateless Way is gateless,

Approached in a thousand ways.

Once past this checkpoint

You stride through the universe.

Buddhism makes mind its foundation and no-gate
its gate. Now, how do you pass through this no-
gate? It is said that things coming in through this
gate can never be your own treasure. What is
gained from external circumstances will perish in

the end. However, such a saying is already raising waves when there is no wind. It is cutting unblemished skin. As for those who try to understand through other people's words, they are striking at the moon with a stick; scratching a shoe, whereas it is the foot that itches.

Wu-men Hui-k'ai, 1183–216 (28)

道

When we are free from attachment to all outer objects, the mind will be in peace. Our Essence of Mind is intrinsically pure, and the reason why we are perturbed is because we allow ourselves to be carried away by the circumstances we are in.

He who is able to keep his mind unperturbed, irrespective of circumstances, has attained Samadhi.

Hui Neng, 638–713 (42)

The Spirit tends towards purity, but the
mind disturbs it.

The mind tends towards stillness but is
opposed by craving.

Lao Tzu, 6th century BCE (7)

Mind is the Buddha. There is no other

Buddha. There are no other Buddhas.

There are no other minds. Mind is pure,

bright and empty, without having any

form or appearance at all. Using the

mind to think conceptually is missing

the essence and grasping the form.

The eternal Buddha is nothing

to do with attachment to forms.

Huang-Po, 9th century CE (41)

'Those who know do not speak; those
who speak do not know.'

Lao Tzu, 6th century BCE (29)

道

According to case 41 of the *Wumenguan* it was the
following dialogue that preceded this awakening
and triggered it:

Bodhidharma sat facing the wall. The second
patriarch who had been standing in the snow, cut
his own arm off and said: 'The heart-mind of your
student has still found no peace. I entreat you,
master, give it peace.'

Bodhidharma said: 'Bring your heart-mind
here, and I will pacify it.'

The second patriarch said: 'I have searched for
the heart-mind, but in the end it cannot be
found.'

Bodhidharma said: 'Then I have thoroughly
pacified it.'

Wu-men Hui-k'ai, 1183–216 (28)

On entering the assembly hall master Huangbo said: 'The possession of many kinds of knowledge is not comparable to the renouncement of searching for anything. This is the best of all things. There are no different kinds of Mind, and there is no teaching, that could be framed in words. Since there is nothing more to say, the assembly is closed.'

Huangbo Duanji, 776–856 (49)

道

Look into your mind and there is no mind. Look at the appearances and appearances have no forms. Gaze at the distant objects and objects do not exist. Understand these three modes of cognition and you will see emptiness.

Lao Tzu, 6th century BCE (7)

There are too many intellectuals in this world

Who've studied far and wide and know a
lot of things.

But they don't know their own original
true nature

And thus are wandering far from the Way.

Even if they explain reality in great detail

Of what avail are all those empty formulae?

If in one instant you remember your
essential nature

The Buddha's insight opens up to you.

Han Shan, c. 8th century CE (38)

道

Through endless ages the mind has never
changed.

It has not lived or died, come or gone,
gained or lost.

It isn't pure or tainted, good or bad, past
or future, true or false, male or female.

It isn't reserved for monks or lay people,
  elders or youths, masters or idiots, the
  enlightened or unenlightened.

It isn't bound by cause and effect and
  doesn't struggle for liberation.

Like space, it has no form.

You can't own it and you can't lose it.

Mountains, rivers or walls can't impede it.

But this mind is ineffable and difficult to
  experience.

It is not the mind or the senses.

So many are looking for this mind,
  yet it already animates their bodies.

It is theirs, yet they don't realise it.

Bodhidharma, 5th century CE (50)

道

If you are able to control desire, then the mind will be still. Clear the mind and the spirit will be pure.

Lao Tzu, 6th century BCE (29)

道

We say that the Essence of Mind is great because it embraces all things, since all things are within our nature. When we see the goodness or the badness of other people we are not attracted by it, nor repelled by it, nor attached to it; so that our attitude of mind is as void as space. In this way, we say our mind is great. Therefore we call it 'Maha'.

Learned Audience, what the ignorant merely talk about, wise men put into actual practice with their mind. There is also a class of foolish people who sit quietly and try to keep their mind blank.

They refrain from thinking of anything and call themselves 'great'.

On account of their heretical view we can hardly talk to them.

Learned Audience, you should know that the mind is very great in capacity, since it pervades the whole Dharmadhatu (the sphere of the Law, i.e. the Universe). When we use it, we can know something of everything, and when we use it to its full capacity we shall know all. All in one and one in all.

Hui Neng, 638–713 (42)

道

This mind, through endless kalpas without beginning, has never varied. It has never lived or died, appeared or disappeared, increased or decreased. It's not pure or impure, good or evil, past or future. It's not true or false. It's not male or female. It doesn't appear as a monk or a layman, an elder or a novice, a sage or a fool, a buddha or a mortal. It strives for no realization and suffers no karma. It has no strength or form. It's like space. You can't possess it and you can't lose it. Its movements can't be blocked by mountains, rivers, or rock walls ... No karma can restrain this real body. But this mind is subtle and hard to see.

It's not the same as the sensual mind. Everyone wants to see this mind, and those who move their hands and feet by its light are as many as the grains of sand along the Ganges, but when you ask them, they can't explain it. It's theirs to use. Why don't they see it?

... Only the wise know this mind, this mind called dharma-nature, this mind called liberation. Neither life nor death can restrain this mind. Nothing can. It's also called the Unstoppable Tathagata, the Incomprehensible, the Sacred Self, the Immortal, the Great Sage. Its names vary but not its essence.

Bodhidharma, 5th century CE (9)

The Six Connectives of Chi-k'ai

1 Reason (*li*): All living beings, down to the smallest insects, have received a moral nature, and have Buddha within them. Constantly resting in this, they attain their perfection, because the gift of reason is equally bestowed.

2 Names and terms: Although reason is the same in all beings, yet in the course of the world, they will not come to the knowledge and use of it, and therefore instruction is necessary to produce belief and remove what is false.

3 Observation of human action: Instruction having been imparted and belief produced, the threefold mode of viewing the world, as already explained, must then be employed.

4 Likeness: Perfection itself being difficult to gain, the likeness to it may be reached.

5 The true development of human nature.

6 Confirmation: Ignorance is for ever gone. The mind becomes perfectly intelligent.

Chi-k'ai, 6th century CE (51)

道

When the mind neither sorrows nor delights, that is supreme attainment of virtue. To succeed without changing is supreme attainment of calm. To be unburdened by habitual desires is supreme attainment of emptiness. To have no likes and dislikes is supreme attainment of equanimity. Not getting mixed up with things is supreme attainment of purity.

The Huai-Nan Tzu, 2nd century BCE (52)

道

When the spirit controls the body, the body obeys; when the body overrules the spirit, the spirit is exhausted. Although intelligence is useful, it needs to be returned to the spirit. This is called the great harmony.

The mind is the ruler of the body, while the spirit is the treasure of the mind. When the body is worked without rest, it collapses. When the spirit is used without cease, it becomes exhausted.

The Huai-Nan Tzu, 2nd century BCE (2)

Confucius said, 'I have heard of flying with wings; I have never heard of flying without wings. I have heard of knowing with knowledge; I have never heard of knowing without knowledge.'

Chuang Tzu, 4th century BCE (2)

Great Stability

Chuang-tzu said, 'Those whose abode is great stability emanate the light of heaven.' The abode is the mind, the light of heaven is wisdom. When emptiness and tranquillity reach the extreme, then the Tao is present and wisdom arises. Wisdom comes from fundamental essence and is not a personal possession; therefore it is called the light of heaven.

It is due to pollution and confusion by greed and craving that people become dull and muddled. When people are confused, wisdom does not arise.

Once wisdom has arisen, one should treasure it and not let intellectualism damage stability. It is not that it is hard to produce wisdom; what is hard is to have wisdom and not use it. Since ancient times there have been many people who have forgotten their bodies, but few who have forgotten their names; to have wisdom but not use it is to forget one's name. Few people in the world reach this, so it is considered difficult.

> Ch'an g San-Feng, various suggested dates
> between 1247 and 1464 (2)

The Fleeting Shapes
of the Physical World ...

How foolish are they who turn away from what is real and true and lasting and instead pursue the fleeting shapes of the physical world, shapes that are mere reflections in the ego's mirror. Not caring to peer beneath the surfaces, deluded beings are content to snatch at images. They think that the material world's ever-flowing energy can be modified into permanent forms, that they can name and value these forms, and then, like great lords, exert dominion over them.

Material things are like dead things and the ego cannot vivify them. As the great lord is by his very identity attached to his kingdom, the ego, when it attaches itself to material objects, presides over a realm of the dead. The Dharma is for the living. The permanent cannot abide in the ephemeral. True and lasting joy cannot be found in the ego's world of changing illusion.

No one can drink the water of a mirage.

Han Shan, c. 8th century CE (25)

道

The Chinese Philosopher is one who dreams with one eye open, who views life with love and sweet irony, who mixes his cynicism with a kindly tolerance, and who alternately wakes up from life's dream and then nods again, feeling more alive when he is dreaming than when he is awake, thereby investing his waking life with a dream-world quality. He sees with one eye closed and with one eye open the futility of much that goes on around him and of his own endeavours, but barely retains enough sense of reality to determine to go through with it. He is seldom disillusioned because he has no illusions, and seldom disappointed because he never had extravagant hopes. In this way his spirit is emancipated.

Lin Yutang, 1895–1976 (26)

The capacity of the mind is as great as that of space. It is infinite, neither round nor square, neither great nor small, neither green nor yellow, neither red nor white, neither above nor below, neither long nor short, neither angry nor happy, neither right nor wrong, neither good nor evil, neither first nor last. All Buddha ksetras (lands) are as void as space. Intrinsically our transcendental nature is void and not a single dharma (thing) can be attained. It is the same with the Essence of Mind, which is a state of 'Absolute Void' (i.e. the voidness of non-void).

Learned Audience, when you hear me talk about the Void, do not at once fall into the idea of vacuity (because this involves the heresy of the doctrine of annihilation). It is of the utmost importance that we should not fall into this idea, because when a man sits quietly and keeps his mind blank he will abide in a state of 'Voidness of Indifference'.

Learned Audience, the illimitable Void of the universe is capable of holding myriads of things of various shape and form, such as the sun, the moon, stars, mountains, rivers, men, dharmas pertaining to goodness or badness, deva planes, hells, great oceans, and all the mountains of the Mahameru.

Space takes in all of these, and so does the voidness of our nature.

Hui-Neng, 638–713 (42)

The Ultimate Truths of Buddhism

For years the dusty mirror has gone uncleaned,

Now let us polish it completely, once and for
  all.

Who has no-thought? Who is not-born?

If we are truly not-born,

[157]

We are not un-born either.

Ask a robot if this is not so.

How can we realize ourselves

By virtuous deeds or by seeking the Buddha?

Release your hold on earth, water, fire, wind;

Drink and eat as you wish in eternal serenity.

All things are transient and completely empty;

This is the great enlightenment of the
    Tathagata.

Transience, emptiness and enlightenment –

These are the ultimate truths of Buddhism;

Keeping and teaching them is true Sangha
    devotion.

If you don't agree, please ask me about it.

So Ch'an is the complete realization of mind,

The complete cutting off of delusion,

The power of wise vision penetrating directly
  to the unborn.

Students of virtue will hold the sword of
  wisdom;

The *prajna* edge is a diamond flame.

It not only cuts off useless knowledge,

But also exterminates delusions.

Right here it is eternally full and serene,

If you search elsewhere, you cannot see it.

You cannot grasp it, you cannot reject it;

In the midst of not gaining,

In that condition you gain it.

It speaks in silence,

In speech you hear its silence.

Hsuan Chuen of Yung Chia, 665–713 (53)

9

ON MEDITATION

When the mind is always empty you journey

from place to place in the country of the
    Buddhas.

When the mind is always moving, you travel

from one hell to the next hell.

Bodhidharma, 5th century CE (50)

道

When you try to stop doing

to achieve being, this very effort

fills you with doing.

Seng-T'san, 7th century CE (50)

Outwardly in the world

of good and evil,

yet without thoughts stirring the heart –

this is meditation.

Inwardly seeing one's

own true nature

and not being distracted from it –

this is meditation.

Hui-Neng, 638–713 (50)

道

Meditation is the reservoir of wisdom,

and the garden of bliss.

Like pure water,

it washes away the dust of desire.

It is armour that protects from evil appetites.

You may not have achieved the state of no-doer,

but you are on your way towards enlightenment

When agitation arises like dust that obscures
the sun,

the rain may dampen it down,

the wind of intellectual insight might
disperse it,

but only meditation will remove it for ever.

Chi-Sha Daishi, 6th century CE (50)

道

Ma-tzu was living as an ascetic and practicing
meditation. Master Huai Jang asked, 'What are
you doing?' Ma-tzu replied, 'Trying to be a
Buddha.' Huai Jang picked up a stone and began
rubbing it. 'What are you doing?' asked Ma'tsu.
Huang Jang replied. 'I am trying to make a
mirror.' Ma-tzu said, 'No amount of polishing will
make a stone a mirror.' Huai Jang said, 'No
amount of meditation will make you a Buddha.'

Ma-tzu Tao-I, 709–88 (50)

Stillness and the Tumbling Mind ...

When the mind keeps tumbling

How can vision be anything but blurred?

Stop the mind even for a moment

And all becomes transparently clear!

The moving mind is polishing mud
bricks.

In stillness find the mirror!

Han Shan, 1546–1623 (54)

道

People perform a vast number of complex
practices hoping to gain spiritual merit as
countless grains of sand on the riverbed of the
Ganges; but you are essentially perfect in every
way. Don't try and augment perfection with
meaningless practice. If it is the right occasion to
perform them, let practices happen. When the
time has passed, let them stop. If you are not
absolutely sure that mind is the Buddha, and if

you are attached to the ideas of winning merit from spiritual practices, then your thinking is misguided and not in harmony with the Way. To practice complex spiritual practices is to progress step by step; but the eternal Buddha is not a Buddha of progressive stages. Just awaken to the one Mind, and there is absolutely nothing to be attained. This is the real Buddha.

Huang-Po, 9th century CE (50)

A Superior Method of Meditation

Not focusing on an opening, not tuning the breath, being utterly empty and silent, not giving rise to a single thought – this is a superior form of meditation.

Chuang Tzu, 4th century BCE (1)

道

The Essential Art of
Sitting Ch'an Meditation

When you are going to sit in meditation, spread a thick sitting mat in a quiet, uncluttered place. Wear your clothing loosely, but maintain uniform order in your posture and carriage.

Then sit in the lotus posture, first placing the right foot on the left thigh, then placing the left foot on the right thigh. The half-lotus posture will also do; just put the left foot on the right leg, that is all.

Next, place the right hand on the left ankle, and place the left hand, palm up, on the palm of the right hand. Have the thumbs of both hands brace each other up.

Slowly raise the body forward, and also rock to the left and right, then sit straight. Do not lean to the left or right, do not tilt forward or backward. Align the joints of your hips, your spine, and the base of the skull so that they support each other, your form like a stupa. Yet you should not make your body too extremely erect, for that constricts the breathing and makes it uncomfortable. The ears should be aligned with the shoulders, the nose with the navel. The tongue rests on the upper palate, the lips and teeth are touching.

The eyes should be slightly open, to avoid bringing on oblivion and drowsiness. If you are going to attain meditation concentration, that power is supreme. In ancient times there were eminent monks specializing in concentration practice who always kept their eyes open when they sat. Ch'an Master Fayun Yuantong also scolded people for sitting in meditation with their eyes closed, calling it a ghost cave in a mountain of darkness. Evidently there is deep meaning in this, of which adepts are aware.

Once the physical posture is settled and the breath is tuned, then relax your lower abdomen. Do not think of anything good or bad. When a thought arises, notice it; when you become aware of it, it disappears. Eventually you forget mental objects and spontaneously become unified.

This is the essential art of sitting Ch'an meditation.

C'han Master Cijao of ChangLu, n.d. (55)

Sitting in Silence

Today I sat before the cliffs

Sat until the mist blew off

A rambling clear stream shore

A towering green ridge crest

Cloud's dawn shadows still

Moon's night light adrift

Body free of dust

Mind without a care.

On the peak of the highest mountain,

the four directions expand to infinity.

Sitting in silence,

no one knows.

The solitary moon shines on the cold
spring.

Here in the spring there is no moon.

It is high in the sky.

Though I'm humming this song,

in the song there is no Ch'an.

Han Shan, 1546–1623 (56)

On the Essential Gateway to Truth

Question: By what means is the root-practice to be performed?

Answer: Only by sitting in meditation, for it is accomplished by dhyana (ch'an) and samadhi (ting). The Dhyana-paramita Sutra says: 'Dhyana and Samadhi are essential to the search for the sacred knowledge of the Buddhas; for, without these, the thoughts remain in tumult and the roots of goodness suffer damage.'

A mind which dwells upon nothing is the Buddha-mind, the mind of one already delivered, bodhi-mind, uncreated mind; it is also called 'realization that the nature of all appearances is unreal'. It is this which the sutras call 'patient realization of the uncreated'. If you have not realized it yet, you must strive and strive, you must increase your exertions. Then, when your efforts are crowned with success, you will have attained understanding from within yourself – an understanding stemming from a mind that abides nowhere, by which we mean a mind free from delusion and reality alike. A mind disturbed by love and aversion is deluded; a mind free from both of them is real; and a mind thus freed reaches the state in which opposites are seen as void, whereby freedom and deliverance are obtained.

Question: Are we to make this effort only when we are sitting in meditation, or also when we are walking about?

Answer: When I spoke just now of making an effort, I did not mean only when you are sitting in meditation; for, whether you are walking, standing, sitting, lying, or whatever you are doing, you must uninterruptedly exert yourselves all the time. This is what we call 'constantly abiding' (in that state).

Hui Hai, 720–814 (57)

Block the passages, shut the doors,

And till the end your strength shall not fail.

Open up the passages, increase your doings,

And till your last days no help shall come to
you.

As good sight means seeing what is very small

So strength means holding on to what is weak.

He who having used the outer light can return
to the inner light,

Is thereby preserved from all harm.

This is called resorting to the always-so.

Lao Tzu, 6th century BCE (58)

道

– 1 0 –

ON HARMONY

The Complete Harmony

In the great beginning, there was non-being. It had neither being nor name. The One originates from it; it has oneness but not yet physical form. … That which is formless is divided into yin and yang, and from the very beginning, going on without interruption, is called destiny. Through movement and rest it produces all things. When things are produced in accordance with the principle *li*, of life, there is physical form. When the physical form embodies and preserves the spirit so that all activities follow their own specific principle, that is nature. By cultivating one's nature one will return to virtue. When virtue is perfect, one will be one with the beginning. ... When one is united with the sound and breath of things, one is united with the universe. This unity is intimate and seems to be stupid and foolish. This is called a profound and secret virtue, this is complete harmony.

The Huai-Nan Tzu, 2nd century BCE (59)

Union with Good Fortune

If one is contented wherever he goes, he will be at ease wherever he may be. Even life and death cannot affect him. How much less can flood or fire? The perfect man is not besieged by calamities – not because he escapes from them but because he advances the principles of things and goes forward and naturally comes into union with good fortune.

Kuo Hsiang, d. 312 CE (60)

· In Harmony with the Age

Heaven, earth, infinite space and infinite time are the body of one person, and the space within the six cardinal points is the form of one man. Therefore he who understands his nature will not be threatened by Heaven and Earth, and he who comprehends evidences will not be fooled by strange phenomena. Therefore the sage knows the far from what is near, and to him all multiplicity is one. Men of old were one with the universe in the same material force, and were in harmony with the age.

The Huai-Nan Tzu, 2nd century BCE (59)

In Harmony with the Mundane World

There has never been a person who has roamed over the transcendental world to the utmost and yet was not silently in harmony with the mundane world, nor has there been anyone who was silently in harmony with the mundane world and yet did not roam over the transcendental world. Therefore the sage always roams in the transcendental world in order to enlarge the mundane world. By having no deliberate mind of his own, he is in accord with things.

The Huai-Nan Tzu, 2nd century BCE (59)

The Height of Virtue

Because of calmness, one's desires will be appeased, and because of harmony, one's impetuousness will disappear. Peace, calmness, and moderation – these are the height of virtue.

Righteousness, uprightness, decisiveness, strictness and firmness of action are examples of strength that is good, and fierceness, narrow-mindedness and violence are examples of strength that is evil. Kindness, mildness, and humility are examples of weakness that is good, and softness, indecision and perverseness are examples of weakness that is evil. Only the Mean brings harmony. The Mean is the principle of regularity, the universally recognized law of morality, and is that to which the sage is devoted. Therefore the sage institutes education so as to enable people to transform their evil by themselves, to arrive at the Mean and to rest there. Therefore those who are the first to be enlightened should instruct those who are slower in attaining enlightenment, and the ignorant should seek help from those who understand. Thus the way of teachers is established.

Chow Tun-I, 1017–73 (61)

The Harmony of Difference and Sameness

The mind of the great sage of India

is intimately transmitted from west to east.

While human faculties are sharp or dull,

the Way has no northern or southern ancestors.

The spiritual source shines clear in the light;

the branching streams flow on in the dark.

Grasping at things is surely delusion;

[175]

according with sameness is still not
enlightenment.

All the objects of the senses

interact and yet do not.

Interacting brings involvement.

Otherwise, each keeps its place.

Sights vary in quality and form,

sounds differ as pleasing or harsh.

Refined and common speech come together
in the dark,

clear and murky phrases are distinguished
in the light.

The four elements return to their natures

just as a child turns to its mother;

Fire heats, wind moves,

water wets, earth is solid.

Eye and sights, ear and sounds,

nose and smells, tongue and tastes;

Thus with each and every thing,

depending on these roots, the leaves
  spread forth.

Trunk and branches share the essence;

revered and common, each has its speech.

In the light there is darkness,

but don't take it as darkness;

In the dark there is light,

but don't see it as light.

Light and dark oppose one another

like the front and back foot in walking.

Each of the myriad things has its merit,

expressed according to function and place.

Phenomena exist; box and lid fit;

principle responds; arrow points meet.

Hearing the words, understand the meaning;

don't set up standards of your own.

If you don't understand the Way right
  before you,

how will you know the path as you walk?

Progress is not a matter of far or near,

but if you are confused, mountains and rivers
   block your way.

I respectfully urge you who study the mystery,

do not pass your days and nights in vain.

Shih T'ou, 700–90 (62)

道

Hexagram 11:
T'ai – Peace

THE TRIGRAMS

above: K'un – Earth, the passive
below: Ch'ien – Heaven, the creative

The feminine creative, which moves downward, is above; the male creative, which moves upwards is below. Thus they combine their influences and produce harmony, so that all things flourish. This is the hexagram that represents the first month of spring.

The Judgement: The small declines, and the great and good is coming. Good fortune and success.

Commentary: Celestial and terrestrial forces are in communion with one another, and all things move freely without restraint. High and low, superiors and inferiors, are combined in social harmony, and, sharing the same aims, are in harmony with one another. Yang, representing strength, lies within; yin representing joyous acceptance, lies without. The superior man is at the centre of things, his fortune steadily increasing, while those of mean nature are at the edges, declining in their intelligence.

The Image: Heaven and earth unite, forming T'ai, the symbol of peace. In such a way a mighty ruler regulates the separate ways of heaven and earth, making the seasons and the divisions of space. So he brings assistance to people on every side.

I Ching, written during the Zhou dynasty, 1122–256 BCE (11)

REFERENCES

Abbreviations:

BTTS = Buddhist Text Translation Society (www.bttsonline.org)

LBG = 'Leaves from the Buddha's Grove' (www.civet-cat.skandinaviskzencenter.org)

OLA = One Little Angel (www.onelittleangel.com)

SDP = Self-Discovery Portal (www.selfdiscovery-portal.com)

STA = Internet Sacred Texts Archive (www.sacred-texts.com)

TCBP = www.texaschapbookpress.com)

TF = www.timothyfreke.com)

VOB = 'A View on Buddhism' (www.buddhism.kalachakranet.org)

ZBHY = Zen Buddhist Order of Hsu Yun (www.hsuyun.org)

1   *Chuang Tzu, Musings of a Chinese Mystic*, Lionel Giles, 1906 (STA)

2   'Tao Te Ching', *Vitality, Energy, Spirit: A Taoist Sourcebook*, trans./ed. Thomas Cleary, Shambhala, 1991

3   *The Huai-Nan Tzu*, trans. Wing-Tsit Ch'an, 1924 (OLA)

4 'Tao Te Ching', *The Chinese Translations*, Witter Bynner, Farrar, Straus, Giroux, New York, 1978, The Witter Bynner Foundation

5 *The History of Great Light* (LBG)

6 *Awakening to the Tao*, trans. Thomas Cleary, Shambhala, 1998

7 *Tao Te Ching*, trans. James Legge, Sacred Books of the East, vol. 39, 1891 (STA)

8 'The Spring and Autumn Annals', trans. Wing-Tsit Chan, *A Sourcebook in Chinese Philosophy*, Princeton University Press, 1963

9 *Zen Teachings of Bodhidharma*, trans. Red Pine, North Point Press, New York, 1987

10 *Tao Te Ching*, trans. Ralph Alan Dale, Watkins, London, 2005

11 I Ching, *The Book of Change*, Neil Powell, Orbis, London, 1979

12 'Commentary on Yin Convergence', *Vitality, Energy, Spirit: A Taoist Sourcebook*, trans./ed. Thomas Cleary, Shambhala

13 Quoted by Lin Yutang in *The Importance of Living*, Heinemann, London, 1938

14 *The Analects*, trans. James Legge, 1893 (STA)

15 *Commentary on the Great Learning*, trans. James Legge, 1893 (STA)

16 Trans. Tony Kline (see Acknowledgements)

17 *The Mencius*, trans. James Legge, 1895 (STA)

18 'Yumengying or Sweet Dreams Shadows', quoted

by Lin Yutang in *The Importance of Living*,
Heinemann, London, 1938

19 'A View on Buddhism' (VOB)

20 'Wen-Tzu', *Vitality, Energy, Spirit: A Taoist
Sourcebook*, trans./ed. Thomas Cleary, Shambhala,
1991

21 Trans. Herbert G Giles, 1845–1935

22 Project Gutenberg's E-text of *A Lute of Jade*,
L Cranmer-Byng, trans. Lionel Giles

23 Trans. Stephan Schuhmacher, © 2009 ENSO
Publishing, Le Montat, France

24 *Garden of Pleasure*, trans. Anton Forke, London,
1912 (STA)

25 *Journey to Dreamland*, Maxims of Master Han
Shan (LBG)

26 Lin Yutang, *The Importance of Living*, Heinemann,
London, 1938

27 *The Silver-White Woman Sutra*, *Buddhist
Tripitaka*, 1st Sutra, trans. Rev S Beal, 1880 (STA)

28 *The Gateless Gate*, trans. Katsuki Sekida (STA)

29 *The Sayings of Lao-Tzu*, trans. Lionel Giles, 1905
(STA)

30 'The Book of Poetry', *Doctrine of the Mean*, trans.
Miles Menander Dawson, 1915 (STA)

31 *The Book of Rites*, *Khü Lî*, Book I, Treatises on the
Rules of Propriety or Ceremonial Usages, trans.
James Legge, 1885 (STA)

32 *The Book of Rites*, *The Than Kung*, Book II,

Treatises on the Rules of Propriety or Ceremonial
Usages, trans. James Legge, 1885 (STA)

33 *The Book of Rites, The Nêi Zeh,* Book X, The
Pattern of the Family, Treatises on the Rules of
Propriety or Ceremonial Usages, trans. James
Legge, 1885 (STA)

34 *The Book of Rites, Kung Yung,* Book XXVIII, The
State of Equilibrium and Harmony, Treatises on
the Rules of Propriety or Ceremonial Usages,
trans. James Legge, 1885 (STA)

35 *The Book of Rites, Hwan Î,* Book XLI, The
Meaning of the Marriage Ceremony, Treatises on
the Rules of Propriety or Ceremonial Usages,
trans. James Legge, 1885 (STA)

36 *The Ethics of Confucius,* trans./ed. Miles
Menander Dawson, 1915 (STA)

37 *The Book of Rites, Shê Î,* Book XLIII, The Meaning
of the Ceremony of Archery, trans. James Legge,
1885 (STA)

38 *Poems from Cold Mountain,* trans. Stephan
Schuhmacher

39 *The Rudiments of Natural Science in China,* Ernst
J Eitel, 1873 (STA)

40 *Wandering on the Way,* Early Taoist Tales and
Parables of Chuang Tzu, trans. V H Mair,
University of Hawaii Press, 1998

41 *The Golden Age of Zen,* Wu Ching-hsiung, 1967
(SDP)

42 *The Platform Sutra of the 6th Patriarch*, trans. Bhikshuni Heng Yin (BTTS)

43 'Sayings', *Vitality, Energy, Spirit: A Taoist Sourcebook*, trans./ed. Thomas Cleary, Shambhala

44 *The Imprint of the Heart*, trans. Henry Balfour, 1884 (STA)

45 'Commentary on Ancestor Lü's Hundred-Charter Tablet', *Vitality, Energy, Spirit: A Taoist Sourcebook*, trans./ed. Thomas Cleary, Shambhala

46 'Clarifying the Way', *Vitality, Energy, Spirit: A Taoist Sourcebook*, trans./ed. Thomas Cleary, Shambhala

47 *Poems by Cha'n Masters*, Series 1, Zen Buddhist Order of Hsu Yun (ZBHY)

48 'The Ultimate Reality Transcends What Can be Expressed in Words', *The Teachings of the Compassionate Buddha*, ed. Edwin A Burtt, 1995 (STA)

49 '*The Record of the Sayings of Chan Master Huangbo Duanji of Yunzhou*' (STA)

50 *The Wisdom of the Zen Masters*, Timothy Freke, Journey Editions, Periplus Editions, Boston, 1998 (TF)

51 'On Chi-k'ai and the T'ien-T'ai School of Buddhism', *Chinese Buddhism*, Joseph Edkins, 1893 (STA)

52 *Tao, The Great Luminant: Essays from the Huai Nan Tzu*, trans. Evan S Morgan, 1933 (STA)

53 *The Song of Enlightenment,* trans. Robert Aitken, The Diamond Sangha, Hawaii

54 *The Autobiography & Maxims,* trans. Upasaka Richard Cheung, paraphrased Rev Chuan Yuan (Ming Zhen) Shakya, Zen Buddhist Order of Hsu Yun (ZBHY)

55 *Models for Sitting Meditation,* trans. Thomas Cleary (LBG)

56 *Poems from the Cold Mountain* (LBG)

57 *A Treatise on the Essential Gateway to Truth by Means of Instantaneous Awakening* (LBG)

58 'The Tao Te Ching', trans. Holmes Welch, *Taoism: The Parting of the Way,* Beacon Press, 1957

59 *Collected Textual Commentaries on The Huai-nan Tzu,* trans. Evan S Morgan, 1933 (STA)

60 'Commentary on Chuang Tzu', trans. Wing-Tsit Chan, *A Sourcebook in Chinese Philosophy,* Princeton University Press, 1963

61 *Penetrating the Book of Changes,* trans. Wing-Tsit Chan (OLA)

62 *The Harmony of Difference and Sameness,* trans. Wade-Gillis (STA)

ACKNOWLEDGEMENTS

I very much appreciated the following for their advice and suggestions and for allowing me access to sources from which some of the texts have been drawn: Art . Ticknor, for The Ch'an Masters section of the Self-Discovery Portal; Tim Freke, for quotations from The Wisdom of the Masters; One Little Angel's inspiring website; The Zen Buddhist Order of Hsu Yun; and Anders Honoré's fascinating website, 'Leaves from the Buddha's Grove'.

I am indebted to John B Hare, host of the incomparable Internet Sacred Texts Archive; Rudy Harderwijk, for the use of texts from his indispensable website, 'A View on Buddhism'; and The Buddhist Text Translation Society.

Special thanks are due to Tony Kline for the use of his translations of *Returning to Live in the Country* 1 and 2, and for *Ninth Day, Ninth Month*, posted on his website www.poetryintranslation.com.

Details of all the above websites can be found at the beginning of References (p. 181).

I am particularly indebted to Stephan Schuhmacher

for his translations of poems by Han Shan and Wang Wei, for his guidance and advice on so many aspects of compiling this book, for access to his remarkable library, and for his admirable Introduction.